THE PORNIFICATION OF AMERICA

The Pornification of America

How Raunch Culture Is Ruining Our Society

Bernadette Barton

NEW YORK UNIVERSITY PRESS

New York

NEW YORK UNIVERSITY PRESS
New York
www.nyupress.org

References to Internet websites (URLs) were accurate at the time of writing. Neither the author nor New York University Press is responsible for URLs that may have expired or changed since the manuscript was prepared.

Library of Congress Cataloging-in-Publication Data
Names: Barton, Bernadette, author.
Title: The pornification of America : how raunch culture is ruining our society / Bernadette Barton.
Description: New York : New York University Press, [2021] |
Includes bibliographical references and index.
Identifiers: LCCN 2020016801 (print) | LCCN 2020016802 (ebook) |
ISBN 9781479894437 (cloth) | ISBN 9781479828340 (ebook) |
ISBN 9781479832040 (ebook)
Subjects: LCSH: Pornography—Social aspects—United States. | Pornography—Moral and ethical aspects—United States. | Pornography in popular culture—United States. | Internet pornography—United States.
Classification: LCC HQ472.U6 B37 2021 (print) | LCC HQ472.U6 (ebook) |
DDC 306.77/10973—dc23
LC record available at https://lccn.loc.gov/2020016801
LC ebook record available at https://lccn.loc.gov/2020016802

New York University Press books are printed on acid-free paper, and their binding materials are chosen for strength and durability. We strive to use environmentally responsible suppliers and materials to the greatest extent possible in publishing our books.

Manufactured in the United States of America

10 9 8 7 6 5 4 3 2 1

Also available as an ebook

For all the Women and Gender Studies students
I have taught over the years.

CONTENTS

Introduction

Welcome to Raunch Culture, USA

In December 2016 president-elect Donald Trump named Andrew Puzder, CEO of the fast food restaurants Carl's Jr. and Hardee's, as his nominee for labor secretary. Puzder is the mastermind responsible for branding the burger chains with advertisements of sexy women essentially making out with food. You may have seen the Carl's Jr. commercial of Kim Kardashian eating a salad with her fingers on a bed, letting creamy dressing drip into her cleavage. In a voiceover she says, "While the best things in life are messy, it's fun to get clean," and then sinks naked into a bubble bath. As she casts a seductive look over her bare shoulder in the tub, a male voiceover growls, "Who said salads can't be hot?" Or you've seen the Super Bowl ad of Kate Upton in a car at a drive-in movie eating a burger that makes her so "hot" she begins crawling over the seats, stripping off her clothing, practically masturbating in a frenzy of sweaty, sexual excitement presumably induced by the pleasure of eating the sandwich. The male voiceover comments, "Introducing the classic patty melt with a spicy twist."

Perhaps you've watched the Carl's Jr. 3-Way Burger advertisement where blonde women strut around a kitchen in white bikinis (reminiscent of their underwear) while wielding sharp knives. The name "3-Way Burger" is, of course, a play on a ménage à trois. In the advertisement, three thin white women with long blonde hair and big breasts cook bacon and feed it to one another provocatively. Figure I.1 shows an image from the opening of the commercial.

Puzder defended his pornified[1] artistic choices, saying, "I like beautiful women eating burgers in bikinis. I think it's very American. I used

FIGURE I.1. Advertisement for the 3-Way Burger, 2016. Source: Carl's Jr.

to hear, brands take on the personality of the CEO. And I rarely thought that was true, but I think this one, in this case, it kind of did take on my personality."[2] Apparently Puzder also imagined that his personality brand of busty white women in bikinis best represented him in a prominent government role. He requested that members of the media use the image seen in figure I.2—a young, thin, blonde white woman with large breasts wearing an American flag bikini holding a burger—when writing about his nomination to serve as labor secretary. The primary responsibility of the US labor secretary is to oversee workplace laws. Consider what this image says about Puzder's vision of the American workforce.[3]

Welcome to raunch culture in the 2020s—when the United States has devolved into a *Hustler* fantasy. Naked and half-naked pictures of girls and women litter every screen, billboard, and bus. Pole dancing studios keep women fit while men airdrop their dick pics to female passengers on buses, planes, and trains. Christian pastors compliment their "hot" wives from the pulpit, and we have whole television programs devoted to "the girlfriend experience"—a specialized form of prostitution. People are having sex *before* they date, and women make their own personal porn to share on social media. Rape and pedophile jokes are commonplace, and those who don't like them are considered prudish. Instagram users measure their self-worth by chili pepper emojis that indicate they are hot and sexy. There are so many topless actresses on the cable series *Game of Thrones*, viewers talk about how empowering it is to see *small* breasts for a change. Hordes of young women prefer the quasi-sex work of being a sugar baby to dating.[4] College parties have costume themes like "CEOs and Office 'Hos." Internet porn drives trends in programming, advertising, and social media, not to mention the technological development of the web. The first lady modeled nude and the "leader of the free world" bragged about grabbing women "by the pussy."

How did we end up living in a cultural scene that might have featured in a pulp story from the 1950s written by a horny science fiction geek, I wonder, and how come so few people even *notice?*[5] In *The Pornification of America*, I answer these questions, explaining what raunch culture is and why it matters. By doing so, I hope to deprogram its conditioning in your subconscious and create some mental space to imagine alternatives. In short, raunch culture matters because it is *sexist*, not because it is *sexy*. It sets expectations that women dress provocatively and appear

FIGURE I.2. Advertisement still of model in American flag bikini, 2015. Source: Carl's Jr.

always "up" for sex while encouraging everyone to sexually objectify women.[6] We see raunch culture *everywhere* in our porn nation.[7] It's on our phones, in the mall, in magazines, movies, and television, in music lyrics and videos, in comedy material, on billboards, bus advertisements, and bumper stickers, on T-shirts, in video games and comic books, in hookup culture, at parties and nightclubs, and in conversations.

Raunch Culture = the Pornification of Everything

Valerie is 21 and biracial (Latinx and white), and it takes her less than one minute to scroll through her Twitter feed before she encounters a picture of a woman's breasts advertising "Celebs who got breast implants on socialshark.com." We are sitting at my dining room table with her close friend Elizabeth, who is white and 20, as I interview both young women about their thoughts on raunch culture. Elizabeth explained, "In the middle of everyone talking, there will be an advertisement for something sexual like, 'Look at this nip slip,' or 'Check out this teenager in her prom picture.'"

Like Valerie and Elizabeth, perhaps you have also noticed a creeping bombardment of provocative, half-naked women in advertisements, social media feeds, and television programming, and wondered *What is going on?* Have you fended off any porn bots? What do you think about the "new college craze of Yeti butting" in which young women model in thongs on Yeti coolers as you can see in figure I.3?

If you shop for girl's or women's clothing, tops are tighter, and skirts are shorter in comparison to clothing norms of the 1970s and 1980s. Try entering a Halloween Express store and finding a costume for a girl or woman that *isn't* "sexy" nurse, "sexy" cat, or "sexy" anything. Perhaps you've seen kindergarteners twerking, or puzzled over the sexual violence portrayed in shows like *American Horror Story*. This is the "pornographication"[8] of the culture, what it looks like when the attitudes, behaviors, and accoutrements once reserved for the sex industry filter into the mainstream. For example, consider the following products,

FIGURE I.3. Examples of Yeti butting, 2016. Source: *Maxim*

activities, and body modifications now commonly marketed: twerking, fake nails, breast implants, push-up bras, long dyed hair, smoky eye makeup, plump lips, Brazilian waxes, platform stiletto shoes (or "stripper shoes"), pole dancing classes for exercise,[9] thongs, and hairless bodies.[10] Porn nation tells citizens: *a sexy girl has the body of a porn star, and knows how to do an epic lap dance for her guy*, while offering her a range of products and services to alter her physical self.

Researchers observed a trend toward pornification in the mid-1990s, a period when media outlets gradually started to represent women as not only impossibly beautiful, but also sexy and DTF (down to fuck).[11] Women had long contended with the "beauty myth,"[12] influencing many to unfavorably compare themselves with models and actresses,[13] but we were not routinely exhorted to look "slutty" and release "our inner porn star" until the early 2000s. Early examples of the beginning of raunch culture include pornography star Traci Lords in a small recurring role in the 1994–95 season of the immensely popular family series *Roseanne*. In 1996 the film *Barb Wire* starring *Playboy* model Pamela Anderson was released, and in 1997 Joe Francis founded the pornographic franchise "Girls Gone Wild" and *Maxim*, "The Best Thing to Happen to Men Since Women," launched its first issue.[14] By

FIGURE I.4. Magazine image of Anne Frank, 2019.
Source: *Harvard Lampoon*

the time journalist Ariel Levy published *Female Chauvinist Pigs* critiquing the rise of pornification in 2005, raunch culture had become mainstream culture. As media scholar Susan Douglas observed, "Young women today have never experienced a media environment that didn't overexaggerate the centrality of sex and 'hotness' to everyday life. This is the way of the world for them."[15]

Indeed, our porn nation encourages consumers to interpret almost *anything* and everything through a sexist, "sexy" lens: burgers, butcher knives, breast milk (see the video "MILF," by Fergie), even the Holocaust. In May 2019 raunch culture hit a new low when the student-run *Harvard Lampoon* magazine published an image of the face of Anne Frank superimposed on the surgically enhanced bikini body of Heidi Montag. The image ran with the text, "Add this to your list of reasons why the Holocaust sucks." News stories criticizing the photoshopped image as "deeply offensive" flooded mainstream media outlets and the *Lampoon* co-presidents and issue editor released a statement apologizing for "any harm we caused."[16] I speculate that the students responsible for creating and disseminating the image did not intend to be anti-Semitic. It's possible they were so socialized into raunch culture, they perceived the picture as a *compliment*.

Toxic Masculinity

Hegemonic masculinity, more colloquially referred to as toxic masculinity—a set of practices that promote the dominant social position of men, and the subordinate social position of women—fuels raunch culture.[17] Toxic masculinity socializes men to use female bodies as currency to enhance their alpha status among men.[18] In turn raunch culture reinforces toxic masculinity, especially men's sense of entitlement to women's bodies. For example among the 67 people I interviewed for this study, Makenzie, who is white and 19, exclaimed, "It makes me sick to listen to people talk!" Six or seven time a day she hears men say things like, "She's hot, I'd do this and this to her." Makenzie clarified, "It's not 'I would love to take her out, or get her something to eat,' it's an 'I would love for her to suck my dick' kind of thing." She further illustrated:

> I had a criminology class last semester. The guy that sat in front of me and one that sat beside him would talk the whole time about a few girls on the other side of the classroom. They thought they were hot and wanted to do stuff to them. I heard one of them say he had a girlfriend, and that she wouldn't be happy about it, but it wouldn't matter.

Like Makenzie, Jordan, who is white and 20, observed her "guy friends" as well as male acquaintances, family members, and strangers casually and continuously sexually objectify women. With words pouring out of her in a fountain of rage, Jordan shared:

> I don't know how many times I see people check other girls out, how many times I've caught people looking at me. I can tell that they're checking me out and it's very uncomfortable. I believe you might look around and think, "Oh that person is attractive," or you might think they're pretty, but don't check out their whole body and stare at them. I had this one guy friend, and we did not stay friends long, because any time we went somewhere he was always checking out girls and their butts. I'm like, "Are you serious? Why are you doing this?" And he would try to laugh it off and be like, "You're just jealous because I'm not doing it to you," and every day he did this, all the time, comparing girls' butts.
>
> There's times I'll be out in public, I'll be leaving a restaurant and a guy will hold the door open for me and I'll kind of glance back and I know he did it just to check me out. It's really disrespectful. I'm even more disrespected that they think I'm dumb enough to not realize what they're doing because I look back and I see it. Every day I literally see men objectifying women even on their way to class, anywhere you walk, like it happens all the time.

Girls and women negotiate overt sexual objectification of the kind Makenzie and Jordan described as well as online misogyny. Angelina said that it is typical for men on the Tinder dating app to rapidly proceed from saying hello to requesting sexy photos. Many send an unsolicited dick pic as "encouragement." Angelina, who is white and 20, said that even when she *politely* refuses to share provocative pictures, many respond with a nasty comment like, "You're too fat to fuck anyway." Such toxic masculinity is visible in individual lives, media entertainment, and the behaviors of those on the national stage. Perhaps you noticed Americans elected a man whose idea of an "entertaining" weekend is having himself, pedophile financier Jeffrey Epstein, and 28 young women flown to Mar-a-Lago Golf Club.

Raunch culture encourages feelings of "aggrieved entitlement" in some men,[19] while social media provides opportunities for like-minded boys and men to form communities built on misogyny, like the "incels." Incel is short for "involuntary celibate," describing men who find it difficult to have sex with women because they believe themselves to be unattractive and/or socially awkward. Elliot Rodger, who murdered six people in California in 2014, and Alek Minassian, who killed ten people in Toronto in 2018, both self-identified as "incels." Kevin, who is white and 43, directly linked raunch culture with this form of toxic masculinity in his interview, saying, "I think the hyper sexuality of raunch culture feeds into hyper masculinity and creates this dangerously potent cocktail of what I should aspire to be, and a level of frustration and self-loathing when I can't obtain these things." Randall, who is white and 29, illustrated this mixture of misogyny and entitlement to women's bodies when describing his high school friend Phil who, Randall said, "only dates 'super thin women,' and not 'fat bitches,'" no matter that Phil is himself unkempt and pudgy.

Origins of Raunch Culture

During our interview Valerie observed, "It's [raunch culture] everywhere but you don't realize. All of a sudden, we're learning there's names for these things and that there was a time that this wasn't. There's always been some sort of sexualization in culture, but it's never been this bad, we just don't realize it." Actually, Valerie is mistaken, but it's not surprising she thinks this given her experience. There has *not* always been a sexualization of culture, nor has the US always been a porn nation, although people have dealt with manifestations of patriarchy for approximately 4,000 years.[20] While valuing women for their youth and beauty is long-standing, the *idea* that women should make themselves sexy for men emerged in the 1920s in the United States.[21] Sociologist Lisa Wade explained that the cultural shift from *courtship* (taking place in a woman's home under the watchful eyes of her mother with the goal of marriage) to *dating* (social activities outside the home with a range of partners) favored the "buyer." Going out required funds that women lacked so thus was born the practice of men paying for women's company. Since the goal in dating, as opposed to courtship, is to go out with many different people, women in the 1920s needed to signal their appeal in a new way to men, and they did so by suggesting a degree of sexual availability.[22]

Liberation movements of the 1960s and 1970s introduced widespread progressive social change. Among these was the sexual revolution—the relaxation of moralistic attitudes about premarital sex facilitated by the invention of the birth control pill.[23] New reproductive tools allowed women greater sexual freedom. As the decades passed, those invested in women's subordination used the internet (among other means) to co-opt and convert the energy, dynamism, and freedom of the sexual revolution into the pale, watered-down, frankly oppressive simulacrum that is raunch culture. Technological developments in the dissemination of pornography aided this sad devolution from liberation to raunch, with new media platforms leading the United States, and other Western cultures, into greater and greater sexualization. Indeed, raunch culture, as we now experience it, was not possible before the digital revolution. New technologies pushed pornography and sex workers from the fringes of the culture to its center.

Finally, raunch culture also marks a media shift from the sexualization of women's bodies as something done almost exclusively *to* women, to an activity also done *by* women.[24] Messengers of pornification tell consumers that "hip" women, like Kylie Jenner for example (see figure I.5), appreciate being seen as sex objects because it is "good" to show off one's sexiness. Media outlets reinforce this by portraying those women who strike pouty poses and say they *enjoy* showing others how hot they are as the most stylish.[25] Constantly told that this state of affairs is *empowering* for women,[26] both women and men enforce the rules of raunch. Bonnie's story describing a night out with the girls after a formal dance illustrates this.

FIGURE I.5. Photo of Kylie Jenner, 2016.
Source: People.com

White, 21, and an ROTC cadet, Bonnie traveled from Kentucky to Central Florida to attend an ROTC military ball in April 2019. After the ball wrapped up, she and her best friend "trekked" back to their hotel room to change out of their gowns and into club clothes for a night out on the town. Bonnie donned a "simple outfit" of a pair of jeans and a "nice top," to then face a room of girls "filled with disapproval." She explained that they perceived the outfit as "cute, but not sexy or hot." Even Bonnie's best friend agreed, saying she wouldn't be "allowed" into the bar crawl area dressed as she was. Bonnie said, "In this situation, I finally understood the societal obligation of being sexy versus presentably attractive and felt limited to what I could or could not wear." Because she hadn't brought any outfits passing the exacting standards of "the mass of girls" in the hotel room, Bonnie created an ensemble out of a mishmash of borrowed clothing. Her revised outfit "consisted of a lacy low-cut tank top, a black miniskirt, and a pair of high heels." She said, "I felt exposed and stripped of my dignity and questioned why I was trying to meet cultural guidelines set by the patriarchy. But I felt obligated to abide by their hotness requirement."

As the girls left to hit the bars Bonnie realized, "I wanted to lie to myself and say that I felt empowered because I had the ability to dress sexy and express my sexuality freely, but I felt constrained. Although I do enjoy feeling and looking 'sexy,' I didn't feel good and couldn't feel comfortable with what I was wearing because I wasn't following my own narrative." When Bonnie questioned the others as to why it was necessary to look sexy, she explained that her qualms "puzzled" them. Bonnie's experience detailed here exactly illustrates what cultural analyst Jaclyn Friedman describes as "fauxempowerment,"[27] as well as illuminates the main lie undergirding raunch culture: when looking sexy is compulsory and controlled by the expectations of others it is, by definition, oppressive and not empowering. Being liberated is something we do because we want to, when we are "following our own narrative," whereas being raunchy is something we perform for others.

A Condition of Inarticulation

As you said "raunch culture," I realized, "Oh wow, this is a name for a thing that is very prevalent in my life, but it didn't have a name before." And not just in my life, but the lives of all the men and women in my generation. All people. So when I think about it, raunch culture is the prevalence of pornographic attitudes and imagery in all public spaces encroaching into private spaces.
—Kayla, 28-year old white woman

Writing and talking about raunch culture is challenging for several reasons. As participants explained, it's "what we're used to," "the way things are," and "our culture." The ubiquity of hypersexualized representations throughout our porn nation normalizes the ideology of raunch, and renders it invisible to many. In simpler terms, raunch culture is the water, and we are the fish. When water is everywhere, we don't notice that we are wet. Perhaps we don't even know we are in

FIGURE I.6. *Sports Illustrated* poster near
Morehead State University Student Center, 2016.
Source: Personal collection

the water, as Valerie suggested, "we simply swim." Take, for example, a photo my graduate assistant snapped for me in August 2016 (see figure I.6).

Someone had hung a *Sports Illustrated* poster of an almost naked model posing provocatively at a staircase descending to our university student center. You can see students walking past it clad in backpacks. Like all student centers, ours is a busy one hosting staff, administrators, faculty, students, and campus guests during a typical weekday. Did anyone notice it as they rendezvoused in the center for a meeting, or grabbed a bite between classes? Or are we so used to seeing images of almost naked provocatively posed women that they barely register anymore? If someone did feel uncomfortable with this image, did they say anything about it? If so, besides the language of religious morality, what *words* might they have used? Americans struggle to find a way to talk about raunch culture because, as I illustrate in the following chapters, we suffer from a "condition of inarticulation" concerning it: we lack commonplace, customarily used language to name, understand, and critique what we see.[28] Even the term "raunch culture" is new to most people.[29]

If finding words to describe and critique raunch culture is challenging, speech that supports it springs easily to mind. As I noted earlier, pornification sells itself to consumers using the deceptive narrative of "female empowerment." This wily frame positions those who critique sexualization as "trying to police women's bodies and control women's sexuality." In my experience when I teach and lecture on raunch culture, some women worry, "I like dressing up and looking sexy. Are you telling me I am bad?" Some men say, "The ladies choose what they wear, and I like seeing boobs." I respond by comparing raunch culture to the forest, and individual decisions to the hiker. It is not up to *me* to decide how any person finds their way through the forest of raunch—maybe stripper heels, the gold standard of raunch, *are* the best shoes on certain terrains.

At the same time, the fact that *some* individuals *sometimes* enjoy wearing stripper shoes does not make raunch culture empowering for women. The complication here is that critiques of hypersexualization are structural while arguments that "women can dress sexy if they want to" are singular *and* both perspectives are valid. Raunch culture is sexist and women should get to pick what they wear. Most people lack the skill and experience to effectively explain this to others. This makes raunch, as Melinda, who is white and 20, said, "a really touchy subject." She elaborated, "I don't partake in it myself usually, but I see a lot of it going on. I think there can be too much of it, but I don't judge people as lesser because they participate in it." Those who are unhappy with raunch culture, like Melinda, face a double bind. She said, "I'm torn between women should not be sexualized and they should be able to look any way they want to. It makes me seem like I'm contradicting myself, but it's hard not to. Women can do it, but raunch culture shouldn't happen."

Melinda is playing a rigged game. She admitted she has a big problem with raunch culture, but also does not want to slut-shame women. Further when she *has* critiqued the sexualization of culture, others called her "judgmental," and this response made her cautious about sharing her ideas in the future.

Finally, even if one brilliantly differentiates structural forces from individual choices while heroically managing not to trigger anyone, listeners *still* may not understand the distinction—especially US citizens who are deeply socialized into individualism—or their eyes may glaze over before the end of the clarification. As discouraging as this sounds, and while it can be an uphill battle at times, challenging raunch culture *is* important. Most of the people I interviewed felt relieved, energized, and personally validated "talking back" to sexist cultural norms.[30] The bright side of introducing those previously spellbound under a condition of inarticulation to a social phenomenon is that once individuals find the words to use, they are hungry to talk about it, and usually have a lot to say.

My Background

In addition to 25 years of teaching students about sex and gender, I am also a scholar on the sex industry. I have researched and published two books exploring the experiences of exotic dancers.[31] The data featured in *The Pornification of America* present insights gained from years of listening to student stories about their lives, and a view of pornification from the perspective of sex workers. Raunch culture glamorizes elements and attitudes of the sex industry urging women to be "good girls gone bad,"[32] with media outlets regularly featuring stories glamorizing "20 Super Hot Actresses Who Have Played Strippers in Movies" and "16 Famous People Who Used to Be Professional Strippers." At the same time that the culture urges young women to be girls gone wild, *actual* exotic dancers continue to suffer terrible stigma. As someone knowledgeable about the realities of stripping, concerned about the

abuses dancers endure, and critical of the economic constraints chan-
neling women into sex work, I perceive raunch culture to be a big con
manipulating women into performing free sex work, into being naked
and half-naked, gratis. To the women reading this considering wearing
incredibly uncomfortable high heels with no arch support that threaten
a twisted ankle and leave welts all over your feet, and tiny little skirts
you can't even sit down in (even while your feet are killing you), who
have bad hookup sex with some arrogant guy forcing his porn moves
on you, I say, consult your inner guidance and prioritize your desires.
Recognize that women historically are *paid* for the aesthetic, emotional,
and sexual labor of sexually arousing and servicing men.

Sex-Positive Feminism

In an Orwellian twist, raunch culture has managed to align itself with sex
positivity, a misreading that does a violent disservice to feminist work
on sexuality.[33] While all feminists agree on certain key issues such as the
existence of patriarchy and the importance of gender equality, feminist
groups differ on their perceptions of sex work. Radical feminists, like the
late Andrea Dworkin, focus their attention on anti-pornography activism, arguing that pornography eroticizes hierarchy, domination, violence,
and inequality, and consider such images symbolic (and sometimes
actual) violence against women.[34] Radical feminists theorize that sex
work illustrates a fundamental inequality between women and men as the
conditions of patriarchy prepare, train, and force some women (usually
poor ones) to sell sex to men for their economic survival. In response,
other feminists, who call themselves sex-radical, sex-positive, and/or anti-
censorship, express concern that a wholesale condemnation of sex work
results in negative consequences for women working in the sex industry.[35]
For example, sex workers, who are mostly women, face greater criminal
penalties when sex work is illegal than do customers, who are mostly men.
    Radical feminists principally concentrate on the institutional conse-
quences of sex work while sex-radical feminists typically explore and

situate individual experiences.[36] To illustrate, on an individual (sex-radical) level, control over one's body means having the freedom to work as a stripper, or not. The income stripping provides may allow a poor young woman to improve her economic circumstances and become financially independent, as was the case for several dancers I interviewed in previous research on the lives of exotic dancers.[37] At the same time, on an institutional (radical) level, most women turn to sex work because they lack other economic options, and suffer under one or more forms of institutional inequality (classism, racism, and sexism). Further, any woman's participation in the sex industry reinforces a sexist social order that negatively impacts all women. While sex-radical and radical feminists are often framed as in opposition, in actuality the sex-positive movement has fought conservative religious organizations more often than it has radical feminists.[38]

Key to sex positivism is the belief that supporting women's pleasure is as important to women's liberation as critiques of patriarchal violence done to women's bodies.[39] Throughout my career I have argued that radical and sex-radical feminism work best in concert.[40] Women require *both* freedom from sexism—the goal of anti-pornography activists and sexual freedom—the focus of sex-positive feminism—to live fully actualized lives.[41] Consumers of raunch culture routinely confuse hypersexualization with sex positivity. This is easy to do for the reasons I have already explored: raunch culture cloaks itself in the language of female empowerment while suffering from a condition of inarticulation. I contend that equating pornification with sex positivity is a form of Orwellian doublespeak because raunch culture is *sex-negative* for the following reasons.

One, raunch culture presents a formulaic, heteronormative version of "hot" female beauty that monolithically features thin, big-breasted, tiny-waisted, and barely clad women with Caucasian features. The ideal sexy beauty represented can include women of color, so long as their ethnicity is framed through a white lens. Consider the March 2017 cover of *Vogue* (see figure I.7), which was accompanied by a self-congratulatory story celebrating fashion's "new racial democratization." According to the author, modern women who inhabit a "borderless, decentralized world are liberated to be themselves, and the options are limitless."[42] Note also the manipulative neoliberal language gushing that 21st-century women have "limitless options" to express their beauty—confusingly illustrated by seven lightly shaded women sporting interchangeable facial features (striking eyebrows, pouty lips, narrow noses, high cheekbones) as well as virtually identical body types. Indeed, the editors even include text on the cover bragging "no norm is the new norm," while displaying a very specific normed beauty. In contrast, sex-positive feminism values the entire spectrum of human sexuality and body type, not restricting itself to the narrow sexuality pornification promotes. As feminist sexologist Carol Queen explained in an interview, sex-positive feminism is the "cultural philosophy that understands sexuality as a potentially positive force in one's life. Sex-positivity allows for and in fact celebrates sexual diversity, differing desires and relationship structures, and individual choices based on consent."[43]

Two, raunch culture is sex-negative because it promotes appearance over pleasure. Looking hot, not feeling good, is the end goal. Beauty scholars like Renee Engeln find that the more women and girls attend to their appearance, *even* when the goal is body empowerment and positivity, the more distressed they feel.[44] The women I interviewed illustrated this, explaining that the heightened body consciousness promoted in raunch culture makes them feel unattractive, unhappy, and unworthy—and this inhibits their experiences of sexual pleasure. For example, Nicole, who is white and 24, said that she feels self-conscious about the way she looks when she is having sex. She explained, "I am thinking about how my thighs look fat from this angle, and I'm not in the moment." In any case, women's actual sexual pleasure is irrelevant within raunch culture, which instead markets the following hegemonic sexist narrative: *it's empowering to be a live sex toy for men.* Compounding this, much of what young people learn about sex comes from contemporary internet pornography, which represents sex through a violent, narcissistic, male gaze.

FIGURE I.7. Models on the cover of *Vogue*, March 2017. Source: *Vogue*

Three, raunch culture enables rape culture, a culture in which rape and sexual violence are common and attitudes, norms, practices, and media normalize, excuse, tolerate, and condone sexual violence. Pornification desensitizes consumers to the hypersexualization of women and girls as Brian, who is white and 25, noted. He said, "It's perfectly normal for guys to comment on women's bodies on social media. Nothing bad is happening to the guys who are doing it and then years of that can lead to attitudes like 'She was dressed a certain way, so I smacked her ass.'" Julia, who is white and 46, argued that there is a thin line between appropriating someone visually and appropriating them physically. She explained, "If your body is there for me to look at, it's there for me to consume. You owe me this, or I have a right. It's not only objectification but ownership of women." Angelina echoed Julia, "Men and especially young college men are so used to viewing women through porn and social media that they then see women as accessible and objectified.

There is a blurring of lines between consensual versus coercion." Thus, as I illustrate throughout this book, raunch culture is also sex-negative because it facilitates rape culture.

Social Location in Raunch Culture

How one is positioned within raunch culture affects one's experience of it. Those who transitioned into adulthood with fewer screens in their lives and fewer oversexualized representations of "normal" are less aware of the content of new media and more concerned with mortgages, families, and the demands of work. Abigail, who is white and 20, illustrated this when discussing her grandmother's relationship to raunch culture. Abigail said, "She is really close to me and she doesn't notice it at all." When I asked Abigail what would make raunch culture visible to her Mamaw, she responded:

> I think it would take a lot of explaining for her to really see it. I'd have to show her. I think she doesn't see it mostly because she's not on social media at all. She's not technologically savvy at all. I think they're [her grandparents] not exactly blind to it, but they have sunglasses on that make it harder to see what's going on. I think they're more concerned with families and going to basketball practice and retirement. I see a lot of raunch culture just going to the mall. But she never goes to the mall. That's more of a younger hangout spot. She doesn't even really watch TV. She just got cable two years ago, and they never have the TV on. She watches *Jeopardy*, but that's about it.

Nor does Abigail's Mamaw play video games or read comic books. Abigail concluded that although raunch culture had a huge impact on *her* life, it was one that her Mamaw did not perceive at all.

Several young people I interviewed shared that when their parents and grandparents *did* encounter manifestations of raunch culture, in a commercial or movie for example, they tended to interpret the representations within the framework of individualism and blame the women. For example, Thomas, who is white and 20, quoted his grandmother who, when watching women twerking in a music video, commented: "Well, I can't believe a young girl would be dancing around and dragging like that, that's uncalled for," or when seeing a Carl's Jr.'s commercial, "Why does that woman need to be in a bikini to eat a cheeseburger?" Like Thomas's grandmother, Angelina speculated that her parents would criticize women's hypersexual dress and behavior and not see the inequality present in raunch culture.

Angelina is a first-generation American in a Russian Pentecostal household. In her extended family, girls marry young, have children, and stay home. Angelina explained,

When I first started college my mom looked me in the face and said, "We don't bless you to go to college," so that was a very hard thing for me to take. If I talked to them about how there's this whole study about girls who act opposite of that [submissive and modest], they're going to be defensive, they're not going to want to talk about it or accept it, they're very conservative. They are very religious, so it's not a topic they're going to want to discuss. They're going to basically say that they [the girls] need to repent and need Jesus and that's the end of that conversation.

While religious identification and participation can be a respite from raunch culture, most conservative religious arguments against hypersexualization stigmatize sexual behavior and attempt to control sexual desire by regulating women's bodies. For example, some conservative Christians advocate "purity" (engaging in sexual behavior only in a heterosexual marriage) and "modesty" in women's dress. Relatedly, Muslim fundamentalists position women who cover themselves completely in burqas as most pious[45] and Hasidism, the most orthodox branch of Judaism, strictly regulates members' dress and sexual behavior. Just as some may resist raunch with religion, others resist conservative religiosity with raunch. It's logical that those rejecting a fundamentalist religious tradition might find relief in the overt sexiness of raunch. I interviewed a young woman who began stripping for just this reason: to rebel against the control her parents and church exerted throughout her childhood and adolescence. The problem is that raunch culture and conservative religiosity are two sides of the same coin.[46] They are both patriarchal cultures of conformity that seek to control women's bodies to be either completely seen or completely hidden, determined not by a woman's personal preference, but in service to men's desires.

As I explore in greater detail in the following chapters, race and sexual orientation also complicate one's experience of pornification. For example, the hypersexualization of women of color in the West predates raunch culture. The subjugation of black women stretches back into the antebellum South, in which it was legal for white male owners to rape black slaves.[47] White supremacy justified this violence by constructing those of African descent as animalistic and oversexed, a stereotype *still* plaguing African Americans in the 21st century. Stephanie, who is black and 50, noted this in our interview. She said, "It did not take raunch culture for black women's bodies to be exploited like this. It always has been. We already know that: the myth about the oversexed African American woman. As a woman who has actually dated white men, I've been told what they expect from me."

Slut stigma also attaches more easily to black and brown bodies than white ones in a racist society, motivating some people of color to be careful and "conservative" in their sexual expression, as Christina, who is Latinx and 26, explained:

Raunch culture with Latinas, it's a hidden mess. I've seen more white cis women participate in it. I know literally one Latina girl who participates. In my experience, it has been mostly white women, or white people. I think it's a culture thing. The culture frowns upon that. We are very conservative when it comes to sex, especially in Latino culture. In my experience, to participate in that, one, your family disowns you, and, two, you're putting shame in the last name. You're putting shame into the family as a whole.

Similarly, in her study of the college hookup scene, sociologist Lisa Wade found that students of color were less likely to participate in hookups than white students, with many seeing hookups as a "white thing."[48] To a woman of color already oversexualized as a "jezebel" or "hot Latina," keeping her shirt on may feel more powerful than taking it off. Further, men of color face more severe sanctions than do white men for perceived or actual sexual aggression, especially toward white women.

While the norms and practices of pornification permeate the entire culture, bleeding into gay male and lesbian spheres, the hypersexualization performed is predominantly a *hetero* sexualization governed by the rules of the "heterosexual imaginary," a form of thinking that "conceals how heterosexuality structures gender."[49] When I began this project, I speculated that raunch culture affected heterosexuals more than queer people. I perceived the study as an exploration of toxic heterosexuality, and saw myself following the leads of scholars who illuminate the hard-to-see workings of dominant groups.[50] To some degree, these suppositions were correct. For example, the hypersexualization of gay male culture predates the internet and operates with a different power dynamic than raunch culture because all the participants are men, although as many will passionately argue, it has its own toxic interplay. And it is true that members of certain groups can more easily opt out of raunch culture than others: older people and lesbians in particular. At the same time, I spoke with millennial and Gen Z lesbians and bisexual and pansexual women who held pornification liable for lowering their self-esteem, creating body image issues, and complicating their relationships with friends and partners. While raunch culture may be more of a "white thing" and a "straight thing," those *most* affected by hypersexualization are young women of any race and sexual orientation.

Why Research Raunch Culture

Before the obsession to make raunch culture visible to people everywhere seized me, I had, for some time, believed that Western culture was failing its youth, especially as regards sex and relationships. A veteran gender studies professor, I have listened as year after year students shared stories that vividly illustrate the negative consequences of abstinence-only sexual education,[51] increasingly violent pornography, bro-culture, and the Instagram arms race to be the most perfect. Over and over, I observed raunch culture to be the root of these and other social dysfunctions. In spring 2013, I made a personal commitment to *do more* about raunch culture after "Deanna" spoke in class.[52] On this particular day, we were discussing rape culture and sexual assault in my course on the sex industry. Deanna, an honors student, a feminist, and a criminology major, shyly said, "I didn't know you could tell men no." She described a "hookup" where she had been lying next to a young man in bed and he penetrated her while she was half-asleep. Deanna explained that she thought she was just supposed to accommodate his desires, and that it had not occurred to her until that moment in the classroom that such an act constituted rape.

Millennials like Deanna, the generation born between 1981 to 1996, and those in Generation Z, born in 1997 or later, manage an omnipresent concentration of sexist representations of women along with the combined challenges of trolls,[53] harassment, assault,[54] internet pornography,[55] hookup culture,[56] dating apps like Tinder, and "dick pics"—a completely *new* cultural norm. Consequently, many struggle with low self-esteem, internalized sexism, misogyny, pressure to be perfect, jealousy, insecurity, stalking, assault, and a lack of romantic intimacy, and blame raunch culture for, if not always creating, at least exacerbating these problems.[57] Teresa, who is 21 and Latinx, summed up what many others observed: our porn nation is a bleak land for women. She said, "Girls just have to be skinny. You have to have big tits, a big ass, and basically you've got to be stupid."

For 20-somethings, raunch culture *is* culture. Born just as the internet began to occupy more and more of our daily experience, Deanna, Brian, Makenzie, Randall, Bonnie, Teresa, and a whole cohort of youth are maturing into adulthood absorbing a steady stream of hypersexualized representations of women in advertisements, music videos, social media, television shows, and movie plots. What effect might this have on how they perceive gender relations? As the folks I interviewed describe in the following chapters, this parade of impossibly thin but curvy, sexy, almost naked female bodies lowers women's self-esteem, heightens their self-consciousness, and complicates their ability to perceive and prioritize their sexual desires.[58]

In the pages that follow, I examine cultural changes in the content of music lyrics and videos, advertisements, television shows, movies, and pornography before people regularly had access to the internet (approximately pre-1995) through the years leading up to the introduction of the iPhone (2007) to the screen-saturated present. Hypersexualized imagery certainly existed before 1995. For example, under the leadership of Helen Gurley Brown, the magazine *Cosmopolitan* featured sexual content as early as the late 1960s; the pop singer Madonna released provocative music videos in the early 1980s, beginning in 1983 with her song "Burning Up"; the music artist Prince produced the album and film *Purple Rain* in 1984; and the band Mötley Crüe released their strip club anthem "Girls, Girls, Girls" in 1987. It is easy to recall such single instances of raunch imagery pre-internet, like the movie *Porky's* (1982) for example, because such illustrations stood out in the cultural terrain. But in the 2020s one can't turn off, stash away, throw out, or put down raunch culture because the images are in too many places, and on too many devices. Raunch culture manifests IRL (in real life), and upon all the many screens that populate our social landscape. Westerners encounter so many sexualized images they cease to be remarkable.

My desire to analyze and critique the US's devolution into a porn nation grew stronger with the 2016 presidential election outcome. I didn't plan this project to intersect with the tail end of the 2016 campaign through the years of the Trump administration, but since it did, I asked those I interviewed to explore if they believed raunch culture played a part in Donald Trump's political ascendance. They had a lot to say. This book includes a chapter discussing how a politician was able to brag about "grabbing women by the pussy," as Trump was recorded doing, and still become president. I will argue that raunch culture deserves part of the responsibility for the election outcome because it normalizes the sexual objectification of women and facilitates a "boys will be boys" acceptance of sexual assault.

"Take It All In"

During our interview Kayla described, and then texted me later, an advertisement she spotted while driving through Las Vegas (see figure I.8) because she thought it well summed up raunch culture She said, "It was 2011 and I saw a big billboard for Studio54. It featured a woman with her head back and her mouth open, a very beautiful-looking woman with big lips and a really big disco ball hanging above her mouth, that is about to go into her mouth and it says, 'take it all in.'" Kayla believed that this image well-captured women's role in raunch culture: to be a hole, a receptacle for other people's pleasure, with no eyes, no voice, and no feelings. She concluded, "I feel like that ties it all together. 'Take it all in,' this is what the world is, you don't have a choice."

Like Kayla, Abigail believes that an important element of raunch involves socializing women to be physically and intellectually submissive to men, in short, to look fuckable and stay quiet: "Not only is everything put on us to change us and the way that we look, but we're also told to be quiet about it and it doesn't matter what we think—that what others think is what's most important." Emily, who is 23 and black, concurred that raunch culture socializes women to be passive and compliant. She said, "They think all women need to look a certain way and be completely submissive, not having a voice or any power. If you have an opinion, it's looked down upon." Bitchy women have opinions. Better for

FIGURE I.8. Studio54 advertisement on Las Vegas billboard, 2011.
Source: Personal collection

women to be bimbos and sex dolls, to fry bacon and wash trucks in bikinis, to care only that men find them hot, to, as Teresa noted, "be stupid."

The Pornification of America explores what raunch culture is, why it matters, and how it is ruining our society. In 2020, state legislatures across the US, including that of Kentucky, where I live and work, are voting to restrict women's access to birth control and abortion, and pushing back the rights of sexual minorities. Meanwhile, messengers of raunch culture encourage young women to be sexy like "porn stars," and feel *grateful* for the opportunity to dress up in stripper shoes, get catcalled, and look at uninvited dick pics because, in the manipulative language of doublespeak, it's "empowering." Raunch culture is a new phenomenon enabled by new media, begging for, in my opinion, more attention and feminist analysis. I hope this book will show you how to better understand, negotiate, resist, and transform fauxempowerment into gender equality.

1

What Men See, What Men Want

Teachers plant many seeds in students, but we don't always see the fruits of our efforts. Not so with the male gaze. There is no other lesson I've found that can so reliably change the worldview of someone in one hour than a lecture on the male gaze, a film theory concept describing what people *see* when watching much Western media. In videos shot from the male gaze, the camera operates like an eye panning up and down women's bodies, sometimes freezing on a woman's breasts or buttocks. In still photography, women pose provocatively, often with much skin showing.[1] Film theorist Laura Mulvey coined the phrase "the male gaze" in 1975, defining it as a way of composing a visual text that privileges the perceived desires of heterosexual men.[2] Mulvey noted three types of looks in her theory of the male gaze: the look of the camera, the look of the audience, and the look of characters within a narrative.[3] A Red Tape advertisement from 2009 illustrates all three kinds of looking (see figure 1.1).

The director of this advertisement constructed the first type of looking—the story the camera tells: three women are center frame, half-naked, on poles, wearing stripper shoes, performing an erotic dance for the businessman. As you analyze this ad, you will observe that your eye is drawn to the women, especially the legs of the woman most front stage. This is the second type of looking. Finally, should your attention momentarily leave the female legs to explore more of the advertisement, the gaze of the fully dressed male character "living *his* fantasy" refocuses your eyes back on the women's bodies. *His* gaze on the women's sexual performance is the third type of looking. In this ad, the male character is the imagined subject and author of the fantasy, and the women sexual objects for his and, by extension, *the viewer's* arousal.

FIGURE 1.1. Red Tape advertisement, 2009. Source: Red Tape

Props Not Characters

Some of the people I interviewed felt frustrated with repeatedly being subjected to the male gaze in programming. Angelina succinctly stated, "Women are being used as PROPS in TV shows and films by oversexualizing them." Thomas, explained that the male gaze created stress in his relationship. Exasperated, he exclaimed, "You can't seem to get away from it, honestly!" Recently married, Thomas doesn't enjoy watching contemporary movies. He specifically brought up the film *Riddick* and the character of Harley Quinn in the movie *Suicide Squad* because both of these stories included gratuitous female nudity that had "no narrative value," and the sexualized scenes of female characters upset his wife. Thomas explained that featuring nude and almost nude women for no reason other than to appeal to an imaginary heterosexual male audience

> Puts a damper on things when you're trying to watch something with your wife and all this overtly sexual stuff starts popping up on TV and

you're like, "Oh, crap." Sometimes it starts arguments. She doesn't like it at all because she has confidence issues, and when she sees a girl on the TV screen naked, or in her underwear overly sexualized, it demeans her confidence. She goes, "Why would you or other men want to look at that instead of you looking at me, or other men looking at their girlfriends that way?"

Not only did such interactions distress Thomas, and cause unnecessary conflict in his intimate relationship, he expressed frustration with the movie industry for manipulating men "into watching a movie because there's a woman in a bikini in it." Thomas, who is an ROTC student and about to enter the military, confided, "That's why I like Disney movies so much, because those are the only movies I can really watch that don't have raunch culture in them very much."

So far I have briefly described the *visual* elements of the male gaze but, as Mulvey theorized, the male gaze also influences content and plot development, in particular *whose* story is told. In narratives controlled by the male gaze, the hero acts while the heroine is acted upon and, while female characters may help the hero transform, they grow little themselves. For example, consider a storyline in which a male protagonist rescues a female character from some danger, like those of the *Taken* franchise starring Liam Neeson. In the films, Neeson's daughter and former wife are supportive characters for his transformation to become a better father and their victimization drives Neeson's journey, not their own narrative arcs. A short list of recent films centering on a "damsel in distress" storyline include *The Dark Knight* (2008), *Deadpool* (2016), *Batman v Superman: Dawn of Justice* (2016), *Jack Reacher* (2012), *Iron Man 3* (2013), *Casino Royale* (2006), and *Sherlock Holmes* (2009).[4] In these, the women are usually subservient to the men in the story, and have little screen time, character development, or lines.

Many movie and television plots also cast female characters as bimbos, bitches, and sex objects. For example, the original *Hangover* (2009) movie features all three of these stereotypes, as does the Spike TV series *Blue Mountain State*. Figure 1.2 shows a poster advertising the series'

FIGURE 1.2. Poster for *Blue Mountain State*, 2010. Source: Spike TV

first season. Several of the 20-something people I interviewed shared that watching *Blue Mountain State* as tweens and teenagers influenced how they behaved with one another. Layna, who is Latinx and Pacific Islander and 20, described the series and its impact in her friend circle:

> They're at a university, and it's following the college football team. The main characters, they objectify women all the time. It's always girls in short, short skirts zooming up on their boobs, and talking about how hot they are. They also throw a bunch of drugs into that, and they party. It's this huge message. Well the guys at my high school loved *Blue Mountain State*, so the girls would be like, "Yeah, look at us, yeah we can do that."

Blue Mountain State premiered in January 2010, and ran for three seasons on Spike TV, which, as many may recall, billed itself without irony as "the first network for men." Netflix made *Blue Mountain State* available to subscribers from 2014 until April 2019, thus expanding its influence to a full decade.

Where Are the Women?

In addition to casting women as sex objects and stereotypes, Hollywood films also routinely *underrepresent* girls and women. According to a study of popular movies in 2015, male characters had twice the screen time of female characters, and spoke two times as often.[5] In films with a male lead, men spoke three times as much as women, and even more often in action films. Oscar-winning films have an even worse ratio of male to female lines. A grim graphic illustrates the gender breakdown in words spoken by women and men in films that won the Oscar for best picture in recent decades (see figure 1.3).

A lack of representation behind the scenes partly explains this inequity, because women hire other women. The *Celluloid Ceiling* study released in January 2019 found that women directed only 8% of the top 250 films of 2018, a number *down* 3% from 2017. Overall, only 20% of

FIGURE 1.3. Ratio of male to female lines in best picture Oscar winners, 1991–2016. Source: BBC

the top-level filmmaking staff—directors, writers, producers, editors, and cinematographers—on these films were women.[6] To understand *why* men dominate Hollywood consider *who* exactly is in charge of making key decision about scripts, casting, and employment in the media industry: titans like Harvey Weinstein (film producer) and Les Moonves (former chairman and CEO of CBS Corporation), both accused in 2017 of engaging in decades of sexual misconduct toward women. A quid pro quo "casting couch" culture setting expectations that men in power *deserve* sex in exchange for roles and green-lighting projects, along with a culture of silence among men about the sexual abuse of women, enabled this predatory behavior. For example, when Anne Peters went to CBS board member Arnold Kopelson to complain about how Moonves had sexually harassed her, Kopelson responded, "We all did that."[7] The same men who feel entitled to sexual favors from women in exchange for work are the ones institutionalizing gender inequality in films and television.

The White Eye

Not only are women and girls routinely underrepresented in film media, so are people of color. Researchers at the University of Southern California conducted a content analysis of 414 screen productions—109 motion pictures, and 305 broadcast, cable, and digital series—in 2014–15 to find that 72% of all characters were white and 28% were characters of color.[8] As the proportion of people of color is 38% in the United States, this representation is 10% lower than the demographic composition.[9] The 2016 Oscar nominations underlined the invisibility of actors of color as *all* those nominated for awards that year were white. In her book *The Hollywood Jim Crow,* sociologist Maryann Erigha details the processes that institutionalize racial inequality and hierarchy in Hollywood. She writes, "As gatekeepers, Hollywood decision-makers actively create and maintain racial hierarchy in how they discuss, conceptualize, package, produce, and distribute movies and in how they stratify movies actors, and directors."[10] Erigha notes that movies with black casts are also systematically underfunded, creating disparities that put such films at a disadvantage throughout their creation and distribution.[11] Further, a single minority of color in a mainstream movie (a token) is often a stereotype (thug, terrorist, gangsta, welfare queen, ho-ho, etc.).[12] Thus, much as women learn to read themselves through the male gaze in media representations, so do people of color see themselves through a "white eye."[13] Black women experience *both* sexism and racism in American visual culture, what feminist Moya Bailey has dubbed "misogynoir."[14]

One can find much misogynoir in some contemporary rap music lyrics and videos although, historically, rap music emerged to further the politics of liberation, not the oppression of black women.[15] A form of rhythmic storytelling, early rap "talked back" to white supremacy by creatively deconstructing social problems like police violence toward people of color and the consequences of poverty in overcrowded urban areas.[16] The late 1980s into the 1990s saw the genre's predominant style change from "message rap"—with lyrics critiquing oppressive power structures—to "gangsta rap"—music that glamorizes crime, drug culture, and elements of the sex industry.[17] Women in "gangsta" rap are largely nameless, interchangeable women of color[18] derogatorily referred to in song lyrics as "hoes," "hoodrats," "bitches," and "chickenheads."[19]

Stephanie, who is black and 50, recalled how the change from message to gangsta rap affected her. She said, "I remember before gangsta rap started coming out. It was cute, innocent, and campy hip-hop." She continued:

> But then the "bitches and the whores" came out, and they started talking about fucking women. The "bitches and the hoes" thing really rattled me. It was very controversial. People were doing it on cassette tapes, and passing it along to other people. It was a beautiful soup for someone who wants to profit. It was sex, it was jarring and also, too, it had an audience that was outside the inner-city audience. White kids liked it and it gave them a peek behind the veil. Provocation sells. I believe that poverty and inequality has a lot to do with why that raunch culture message first came out of the very poor urban black experience.

FIGURE 1.4. Screenshot of "Tip Drill" video by Nelly, 2000. Source: Universal

Stephanie concluded, "It is very, very disturbing to me as a black woman." The video for Nelly's "Tip Drill" (2000) well illustrates "gangsta rap." In it, men throw money on women's bodies while they mimic sex acts. The video ends with Nelly swiping a credit card down a woman's buttocks. Capitalism, patriarchy, white supremacy, and raunch culture intersect in gangsta rap—music lyrics and videos exploit a black urban experience to profit mostly white male executives[20] while furthering the politics of racism and patriarchy.[21] As filmmaker Sut Jhally notes in *Dreamworlds 3*, the depiction of black men as thugs and criminals, and black women as bitches and hoes, in many rap videos constitutes the most racist set of cultural images since the early 20th century.

"You Will Never Look at TV the Same Way Again!"

Often invisible to viewers until they learn about it, once seen, the male gaze cannot be unseen. When I teach about it, I ask students who have had the lecture before to share what their classmates may expect. They laugh and groan and shake their heads. They say, "You will never look at TV the same way again!" After I inquire where they see the male gaze, the students respond in chorus, "Everywhere!" Heather, who is white, 22, and one of my former students, explained that once she was aware of the male gaze, negotiating movie and television choices with her ex-boyfriend was a struggle. She was one of several people who brought up the HBO series *Game of Thrones* to illustrate the male gaze, misogyny, and raunch culture. Heather shared, "My ex, one of the things he got really upset about was that I tried watching a few episodes of *Game of Thrones* and there were so many sex scenes. The sex scenes were just straight-up pornography, there was no way around it. It was just so misogynistic, it was really sickening and I felt super nauseous sitting there watching the first ten minutes of an episode." Kayla, from the last chapter, stopped watching *Game of Thrones* after the first season. She bitingly observed, "If the *Game of Thrones* is on, almost every time you walk in the room some young, beautiful actress playing a prostitute is sleeping with some old, nasty guy. It's gratuitous, almost faceless naked women walking around for the purpose of showing that these guys are sleeping with attractive women. They don't even have any lines. Why are they there?"

Because viewers see so many images shot from the male gaze, they embed themselves in our subconscious minds naturalizing a gender hierarchy in which men do the looking and women pose provocatively.[22] Several people, like Kimberly, who is white and 26, believed that the male gaze affects them on a "subconscious level." Kimberly said, "It's constantly in the back of my mind thinking through everything that I'm doing and never really being comfortable doing what I want to do, or saying what I want to say, wearing what I want to wear." The images from shows like *Game of Thrones*, the *American Pie* movies, the *Hangover* films, music videos, and Instagram posts, as well as Hardee's commercials, perfume ads, and so on, endlessly, *work together*, as media scholar George Gerber theorized, to "cultivate" the viewer's understanding of the social world.[23] Cultivation theory explores how continuous exposure to a set of messages over time subtly influences the way viewers perceive reality. Consumers rarely consider that directors and producers *create* sexist images and narratives through a chain of multiple choices.[24] For example, we don't know about the stream of projects Les Moonves rejected at CBS, nor how his sexual misconduct, like a quid pro quo expectation of oral sex for work,[25] biased nightly television programming on the network from 1995 to 2019. Instead, most of us read media as a *natural* rendering of social life.

In the following few pages, I will attempt to make the natural unnatural; in other words, make visible the male gaze in a variety of media platforms including cartoons, video games, comic books, television, music videos, advertisements, movies, and social media beginning in 1943 up to 2019, with the goal of encouraging you to consider the impact of these images. In addition to noting elements of the male gaze as you analyze these, please also observe how the images grow more pornified over time.

FIGURE 1.5. Still from *Red Hot Riding Hood*, 1943. Source: Metro-Goldwyn-Mayer

FIGURE 1.6. Seventeen cosmetics advertisement. 1947. Source: *Cosmopolitan*

FIGURE 1.7. Still of Marilyn Monroe in *River of No Return*, 1954. Source: 20th Century Fox

FIGURE 1.8. S.O.S advertisement, 1956. Source: S.O.S

FIGURE 1.9. Broomsticks pants advertisement, 1967. Source: News Dog Media

FIGURE 1.10. *Thunderball* advertisement, 1965.
Source: Alamy

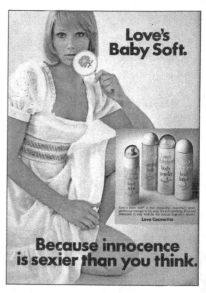

FIGURE 1.11. Love's Baby Soft
advertisement, 1970s.
Source: Wordpreneur.com

FIGURE 1.12. *Dynasty* cast photo, 1980.
Source: ABC

FIGURE 1.13. Brooke Shields in Calvin Klein jeans
advertisement, 1980. Source: Calvin Klein

FIGURE 1.14. Panel from *Wonder Woman* comic, 1987–2006.
Source: DC Comics

FIGURE 1.15. Still from *Who Framed Roger Rabbit*, 1988.
Source: Touchstone Pictures

FIGURE 1.16. Still of Princess Jasmine in *Aladdin*, 1992. Source: Disney

FIGURE 1.17. Still of Pamela Anderson in *Barb Wire*, 1996. Source: PolyGram Filmed Entertainment

FIGURE 1.18. Screenshot from the *Dead or Alive* game series, 1996–2016. Source: Tecmo

FIGURE 1.19. Poster for *Lara Croft: Tomb Raider*, 2001. Source: Paramount Pictures

FIGURE 1.20. Marvel heroine in *Red Sonja* advertisement, 2005. Source: Marvel

FIGURE 1.21. Tom Ford for Men advertisement, 2007. Source: Tom Ford

FIGURE 1.24. Lola Bunny on the *Playboy* cover, 2011. Source: *Playboy*

FIGURE 1.22. Shia LaBeouf and Megan Fox in *Transformers*, 2007. Source: DreamWorks Pictures

FIGURE 1.23. "Shameless" advertisement by Suit Supply, 2010. Source: Suit Supply

FIGURE 1.25. Screenshot from *Duke Nukem Forever*, 2011. Source: 3D Realms

FIGURE 1.26. Still from Robin Thicke video "Blurred Lines," 2013. Source: Star Trak/Interscope

FIGURE 1.27. Still from Miley Cyrus video "Wrecking Ball," 2013. Source: RCA Records

FIGURE 1.28. Still of Margot Robbie and Leonardo DiCaprio in *The Wolf of Wall Street*, 2013. Source: Paramount Pictures

FIGURE 1.29. Still of Alice Eve playing Dr. Carol Marcus in *Star Trek Into Darkness*, 2013. Source: Paramount Pictures

FIGURE 1.30. Advertisement for the Nicki Minaj single "Anaconda," 2014. Source: Young Money

FIGURE 1.31. Screenshot of Hannah Ferguson in Hardee's "I Love Texas" commercial, 2014. Source: Hardee's

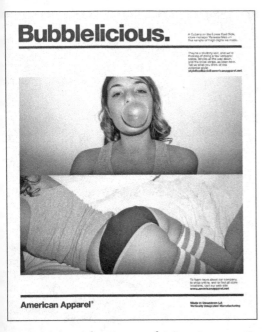

FIGURE 1.32. Advertisement for American Apparel clothing, 2015. Source: American Apparel

FIGURE 1.33. Still of Harley Quinn, played by Margot Robbie, in *Suicide Squad*, 2016. Source: Warner Bros. Pictures

FIGURE 1.34. Still of Emilia Clarke as Daenerys in *Game of Thrones*, 2016. Source: Warner Bros. Pictures

FIGURE 1.35. Model in Calvin Klein advertisement, 2016. Source: Calvin Klein

FIGURE 1.36. Photo of 23-year-old Carina Linn, dubbed the "World's Sexiest Nurse." Source: Instagram

FIGURE 1.37. Photo of Dan Bilzerian, dubbed the "Instagram Playboy King," 2018. Source: Instagram

22 Hot Instagram Models Who Are Also YouTube Stars - YouGoDe 2019

FIGURE 1.38. Screenshot of Instagram models and YouTube stars, 2019.
Source: YouGoDe

Bro-Privilege

What are the consequences of growing up, living in, and negotiating social environments saturated with the male gaze? I argue that early and repeated exposure to the male gaze acclimates Westerners to raunch culture and helps groom women for androsexism, "a type of 'sexism' biased in favor of 'male' identified persons, concepts, and practices."[26] Androsexism is a new form of sexism that permits girls and women a small amount of compromised power, what I describe here as "bro-privilege," when they temporarily become "one of the guys."[27] Bro-privilege allows women to enter into and participate in male-centered and dominated environments like online gaming and strip clubs to the degree that they conform to the rules of hegemonic masculinity.[28] One reason girls and women adopt bro-privilege is, as participants like Valerie explained, "so guys will think you are hot and cool." Kayla said: "The women who are cool are cool because they're like 'one of the guys' or they're cool because 'oh I'm not uptight and prudish like all those other women.'"[29] Thus, where traditional sexism fixes women as the object of the male gaze, bro-privilege allows girls and women to temporarily wield the male gaze as honorary men.

Privilege is a set of unearned advantages majority group members hold within systems of inequality. Privilege is linked with one's social location, including but not limited to one's race, class, sex, gender expression, sexual orientation, religion, region, appearance, and ability level. Typically, privilege benefits majority members within an axis of inequality. For example, men have male privilege and white people race privilege. Bro-privilege is a *pseudo* privilege because it is both precarious and temporary compared to other forms of privilege. Men who benefit from male privilege and white people from white privilege do so whether they want to or not because being male and being white are *ascribed* (we are born into these) identity categories. One cannot shed male or white privilege. For example, a man who is opposed to sexism and who critiques his privilege, who speaks up for the rights of women and girls, continues to benefit from male privilege. In contrast, a woman or girl's ability to wield bro-privilege is dependent upon, one, not challenging gender hierarchies,[30] and, two, how the men around her receive it. *They* decide if she gets to be an "honorary guy," and they decide when she doesn't. Should a man perceive a woman wielding bro-privilege as "uptight," "demanding," or "prudish," he can demote her from "dude" to "bitch" status with a single comment.[31]

The evolution of sexism to include androsexism offers evidence that feminist ideas about gender equality have influenced societal expectations of gender norms. It is commonplace in the 2020s that women go to college, pursue professional careers, and play sports, for example, activities which, until the 1960s, were mostly reserved for men. But, while feminist ideas about women entering male-dominated arenas have gained some cultural traction, the reverse is not the case. Western societies permit women much more leeway to be "like a man" than men to be "like a woman,"[32] policing and punishing men who engage in any behavior coded feminine, and femininity itself continues to be stigmatized.[33] Indeed, femininity is so despised, bro-privilege offer girls and women a respite from the "humiliation" of being female.

Women allying themselves with masculine power is not a new phenomenon. For example, Kimberly, said that she learned her "defeatist perception of girls" from her mother. She explained:

> She's always had very precarious friendships with women. In high school she told me horror stories about the very stereotypical, "That girl stole my boyfriend, my boyfriend cheated on me with my best friend." I was just like, "Ugh, I don't like girls, I'm only going to be friends with boys." She's always told me, "I'm a guy's girl, I'm not a girl's girl," and hearing things like that—not just from her, but from a lot of people, "I'm a guy's girl, I'm not a girl's girl," plants a seed in your brain like, "Am I going to be a guy's girl or a girl's girl?"

You have likely heard women say something similar (or identical) to this in your daily life. Since we are all socialized to support patriarchal power structures,[34] and most of us want pleasant conversational interactions, when a girl or woman says, "I prefer guy friends over girls—too much drama," or "Women bosses are the worst—so backstabbing," most of us nod our heads and smile. We may even chime in with a story of an awful female we know. Majority groups facilitate and encourage minority members attacking *each other* like this because such "horizontal hostility" upholds their power.[35] But, if socializing women to put down "mean girls" and "female bosses" and "mothers-in-law" and "hookers" is business as usual in patriarchy, what has changed in this androsexist time is the expectation that heterosexual women assert dominance over other women by sexually objectifying them.

Participants explained that it is common for a young woman to buddy up with her guy friends, "who are," one shared, "better to hang out with than other women," and agree with *the guys* that so-and-so is a 10, "in fact she's so hot, I'd do her." My student Caroline explained this to me in the classroom one day when I shared a personal story about a date's loutish behavior. We were discussing catcalling. I recalled going out with a young man when I was 16 who hollered "nice legs" at a woman walking on the street *while I was in the car with him*. Even my pre-feminist 16-year-old self recognized this as problematic behavior, and I gave him a "you are an ass" look. Caroline said that now boys expect girls to agree with them. In other words, young women are trained to respond, "Yes, she is sexy. I'm usually straight, but she's so hot I could tap that too."[36]

Angelina explained in our interview that it is normal for young women to evaluate other women's bodies and sex appeal. She used to do it herself:

> When watching movies, male friends of mine say something along the lines of "Wow she's sexy" or "Look at her legs," or her butt or her boobs. They wouldn't outright say they would bang her or anything, but do not hold back in making comments about the character's sexual appearance and sexuality. Even a few years ago I would also participate by acknowledging that the woman in the movie was sexy or hot and she looked good, which may very well be, but now I recognize the incredible sexism that exists in films like that.

Thomas observed men validate women who talk about how "hot" another woman is. He said, "I hang out with 20-year-olds and that's how they act. If a girl comes up to them and says, 'I think that girl looks hot because she is in a bikini,' they'd be, 'Oh heck yeah, girl!' Then give her a fist bump and chug a beer with her." Jody, who is white, 18, and a lesbian, observed heterosexual women sexualizing her and one another. She said, "I've had straight girls be like, 'Wow, Jody, why do you got to be so sexy?' or something. They'll hypersexualize each other, and I'll be 'Hey, can you calm down?'" When I updated my research on exotic dancers, one of the big new findings was that the number of heterosexual women visiting strip bars had increased. Club managers put the share of female customers at 40% on weekends, a huge rise from 15 years ago. Dancers also described female customers shouting "Show me your pussy" as they performed on the main stage.[37] As much as I would like to think that these homoerotic declarations signal women's real attraction to *one another*, most of the time they do not. Instead, such statements illustrate *desire for bro-privilege*, not *desire for women*.[38]

By adopting the male gaze and assuming bro-privilege, a woman becomes a *subject*—a dude—rather than an object—a sex doll. As Ariel Levy notes in her book *Female Chauvinist Pigs*, sometime women do both simultaneously: they sexually objectify other women as honorary dudes while displaying their own sexy appeal. I observed this in strip bars when female customers took their own tops off while commenting on the sexiness of the dancers. Popular culture sometimes, confusingly, encourages women to be both sex doll *and* bro at the same time as seen in figure 1.39. Here, we see an almost naked woman so self-absorbed with her own potential sexy appeal that she photographs her crotch while a lion stalks her, and this is both "stupid" and "ballsy" (itself an androsexist term). It is also, most obviously, *for men*. Linguistically, this ad positions the model simultaneously as stupid, an object to desire, and one of the guys. Infuriatingly, the Diesel "Be Stupid" ad campaign won the Grand Prix award in Cannes in 2010. The jury praised Diesel for its "bravery."[39]

I understand the seductive appeal of bro-privilege. It offers women and girls some relief from subordination and objectification—the opportunity to be "balls to the wall" like the lads. It also allows girls and women whose appearances do not fit cultural ideals of size, race, disability, age, and/or gender expression access into otherwise closed social circles, as well as a role to play. For example, the large-sized girl may not be the desired object of the male gaze, but she can play the funny sidekick rating other girls on how hot they are, and dissing those who "try too hard" or wear "skanky hooker heels." Likewise, a black woman can seek relief from misogynoir through bro-privilege, although negotiating the double burden of racism and sexism makes her status as "dude" even more unstable than a white woman's. Finally, it is important to distin-

FIGURE 1.39. Example of Diesel "Be Stupid" ad campaign. Source: Diesel

guish bro-privilege from queer "female masculinity," or butch gender expression. In a queer egalitarian framework no gender expression is valued over any other, e.g., femme is equal to butch, not subordinate to it.[40] So where the lesbian (and heterosexual) butch gender expression undermines patriarchal gender roles, the straight woman assuming bro-privilege sustains them. The butch lesbian *embodies* her gender identity while the heterosexual woman *performs* masculinity.[41]

Both the male gaze and androsexism prop up raunch culture, a system that allows women the following narrow and compromised forms of power: to be admired for looking sexy, and the opportunity to temporarily stake out a position of superiority over other girls and women by claiming bro-privilege. In the rigged game of raunch culture, it makes sense that women use any available tactic to momentarily increase their personal control, including androsexist ones. At the same time, it is also important to recognize that conceding to the terms of an androsexist "patriarchal bargain"—accommodating patriarchal norms that disadvantage women as a group to maximize one's personal gain—undermines women's collective power.[42] In other words, the ability to assume the male gaze and be "one of the guys" does not equal liberation, nor does it exempt women from sexist abuse and degradation. Further, with new technologies come new sexist consequences.

2

How Internet Pornography Ruins Sex

I remember the first time I saw pornography. It was the summer of 1985. I was 18 years old and had just completed my first year at Oberlin College. My stepfather's new job had moved the family from coast to coast, from Framingham, Massachusetts, to Milpitas, California. It was a little bit of a boring summer for me, too short a period to make any real friends, and completely out of context with the rest of my life. I worked as a cashier in a record store for minimum wage and, newly vegetarian, ate a lot of bean tostados from Taco Bell. My favorite recreation was to ride a ten-speed bike to the trails in the California hills and hike alone. Capering along the paths, I felt like a woodland sprite, chomping on fresh fruit grown in our backyard while drinking unconcernedly from the clean streams flowing all around me (miraculously, I never contracted giardia).

I don't recall ever seeing any other people during these hikes, and it never occurred to me to consider my safety until I came across a pornographic magazine all alone in the woods. Some flapping pages on a rock aside one of the streams caught my eye as I danced along the trail. Curious, I descended to the water to investigate. It was hardcore pornography, 1985-style, not glossy *Playboy* centerfolds, but many photos of naked people and penetration. I really don't recall the specific images so much as the feeling of being repulsed by the photos and suddenly, acutely aware of how alone I was in the woods. Some man (I assumed) had brought this magazine to this secluded spot, presumably to masturbate. I quickly scanned the area—was he still around, watching me find it? I didn't spot anyone and, thoroughly creeped out, swiftly left the park. I returned to find my bicycle vandalized, the front wheel stolen off it while I had been away. That was the last time I hiked alone in the

California hills, or even hiked at all in Milpitas. I left the following week to return to college, but I know I wouldn't have returned to the trail alone, polluted as the place had become by the threat implied in the images I had seen: women are objects to penetrate, and I was a woman, ergo, I was vulnerable.

The ease of accessing internet pornography means that most children see pornography much younger than I did. Studies find that over 95% of children have seen pornography before age 18.[1] Some cite 11 as the average age of first viewing.[2] A recent analysis of male consumption of pornography found that 59% of men look at porn weekly and 49% first viewed it before age 13.[3] Two-thirds of those I interviewed saw pornography for the first time online, between the ages of 11 to 13, and some even younger than that. Makenzie first saw pornography when she was seven years old. She explained that she had spent that summer playing with other children in her subdivision. One day, when she was over at her best friend's house in the computer room, a nine-year-old neighbor boy began searching "big boobs" and "saggy boobs" on the family computer. Up popped internet pornography. Makenzie said she "was in shock and went home to tell my mother everything." This was in 2005, a time when internet pornography was widely accessible, but before the release of the iPhone in 2007, the iPad in 2010, and the Kindle Fire in 2011.

Although most machines allow parents to filter the content and "lock down" internet access, if a parent neglects to do this, children may accidentally see pornography as they click links and videos on their mobile devices. Julia, who is white and 46, shared that she found a dozen hardcore porn videos downloaded onto her nine-year-old daughter's Kindle Fire. Julia explained:

> We had given her a Kindle and I had not put any controls on it yet. There were a dozen hardcore porn videos downloaded on it, the same one 12 times. I went to her search history and it started off with something on YouTube, "Justin Bieber hugging a fan," and then you get those

thumbnails on the side, and from that it stair-stepped to this porn video. I erased all of them. It wasn't very long, it was five minutes, but I remember thinking, "Is she searching these terms?" It went from Justin Bieber hugging a fan to Justin Bieber giving a fan a kiss, to Justin Bieber and Selena Gomez, it's how these YouTube videos get categorized. There are thumbnails on YouTube, and you can access videos that are similar to it. It was this progression and so I thought, "Yeah, this is how they hook you in with Justin Bieber, who is marketed for kids."

About half to two-thirds of the young people I interviewed came across pornography accidentally, like Julia believes happened with her daughter. While most of the young people I interviewed did not actively seek out the first pornography they saw, motivated children and teens can easily watch porn on someone else's device, or, if they are technologically savvy, circumvent the parental controls on their own machines.

When adults are too squeamish or puritanical to engage in educational conversations about basic anatomy and sexual pleasure with young people, tweens and teenagers turn to internet pornography to answer their questions. Courtney, who is white and 20, told me a story about a friend trying to share sexual information with a young woman who "had never had sex" and did not know "what all the holes were." To avoid "being awkward" they "resorted" to internet pornography to show her where to find the vagina and anus. Courtney said, "That was kind of a bad decision because then we were all grossed out, because gross things happen on porn. We were trying to find something without violence, so we tried masturbation things, but even those were gross." Finding out about sex from pornography would be fine if the content were not so relentlessly sexist, and weirdly violent, or as Courtney described, "gross."

Raunch culture is the offspring of pornography, thus, the sex industry sets standards for what is "sexy" and "hot."[4] I am interested in exploring representations of "hot sex" in internet porn to consider both what is filtering into mainstream culture via porn, and the consequences of these images in the lives of children and young people. As I see it, there are four major problems with internet pornography: it is too easy for children to access; the content is unrealistic and sexist; it pushes the envelope of mainstream programming; and we lack the conversational tools to make sense of it with one another. Like raunch culture, internet pornography is problematic not because it is *sexy* but because it is *sexist*. The analysis of pornography I advance here is neither a condemnation of sexual behavior nor sexual images, but instead a critique of oppressive representations. What we need in place of internet pornography, or at least alongside it, are more conversations about women's sexual pleasure.

Technologies of Pornography

The cost of technology that "improves" faster than humans can process is nowhere more visible than in internet pornography. Something weird and "creepy," in the language of millennials, is going on with the content of internet porn and it behooves us to pay attention.

Pornography is visual or print materials of sexual activity intended to arouse consumers. The medium through which people view pornography has evolved over time with the introduction of new technologies— from erotic art to photography to moving pictures to the internet. A century and a half ago pornography consisted of black and white photographs of erotic scenes on playing cards, postcards, and cabinet cards. Perhaps a man kept these hidden under the bed, or in the backyard, or in a box in a woodshed. Film technology introduced the "blue movie." These first pornographic films were silent films shown in some brothels in the 1920s, later progressing alongside their talking picture counterparts into "XXX-rated" films shown in sticky theaters.[5] Interested customers could also visit sex shops to watch pornographic shorts running in a constant loop in coin-operated single-person booths.

In the late 1970s innovative VHS technology allowed people to watch pornography in the solitude of their own homes, and, as might be expected, this new privacy encouraged more pornography consumption.[6]

The market transition from VHS to DVD in the 1990s offered customers improved visual and sound quality as well as "extra features," like commentary from the director and interviews with actors. The change from analog to digital technologies gave porn a new medium: the internet. The introduction of streaming technologies and the smartphone enable viewers to watch pornography on their computers and mobile devices. Today, pornography creation and transmission not only matches the pace of internet connectivity, one can make a fair case that market demands for innovations in pornography *drive* the social and technological development of the web.[7] This rapid technological expansion means that pornography is now easier to find and access than at any other time in human history.[8]

As I discussed earlier, radical feminists have been critically analyzing and condemning the representation of women in pornography for over 40 years, well before internet pornography and the introduction of the handheld device.[9] As decades of feminist research and analysis substantiates, the majority of pornography is both sexist and misogynist: it demonstrates hatred for women while normalizing women's sexual submission and service to men.[10] Most internet pornography cast women as always-willing sex partners turned on by any and all acts, including violent ones.[11] Of course, one can find violence in some pre-internet porn—and moreover, representations of any group that routinely subordinates them is symbolic violence—but, as I will shortly elaborate, it is commonplace to see violence done to women in internet porn. For example, a 2010 study published in the journal *Violence Against Women* counted acts of physical and verbal aggression in 304 scenes from the most popularly viewed pornography. The data show that 88% of scenes contained physical aggression and 48% verbal abuse.[12]

Egalitarian porn does exist. American producer and director Candida Royalle founded Femme Productions in 1984, and Swedish film director, producer, and screenwriter Erika Lust created LustFilms in 2004, both with the goal of creating pornography centered on female desire. Calling their genre "feminist pornography," Femme Productions, LustFilms, and websites like Lady Cheeky present women and men more realistically and feature sex acts that women almost universally find pleasurable, like cunnilingus. While I support, and applaud, the efforts of some to create egalitarian pornography, this content does not solve the problem of sexism in internet porn because feminist porn is a niche. Feminist porn sites will not appear at the top of, or in the first page of results, in a general Google search for pornography. A user has to know that feminist pornography exists at all to search for it, and many consumers have had neither the sexual nor gender studies educations to knowledgeably do so, certainly not children and teens. What they *will* find easily, at best, are acrobatic acts that center male pleasure, and, at worst, porn depicting sexualized violence against women.

Porn Is Everywhere

Considering accessibility, to test how easy it is to find pornography with a child's search term, I followed the lead of Makenzie's childhood friend and typed "boobs" into Google to see what might come up in November 2017. The very first link on the page was titled "Big Boobs (.Y.) Big Tits Official Site." Clicking on the link, I found dozens of thumbnail videos I might instantly play, all of which were graphic. If none of these pleased me, the site allowed me to search by categories helpfully supplied in an A–Z menu: Amateur, Anal, Asian, Babes, BBW, Blowjob, Ebony, Group, Hardcore, Latina, Lesbian, MILF, Natural, POV, Solo, and Teen (18+). As I dutifully typed the categories here, I realized I wasn't entirely sure what "POV" was and clicked on it. The thumbnails featured camera angles of women with eyes bulging, mouths stretched wide barely covering huge penises. While reasonably convinced that POV was short for "point of view," to make certain, I typed into Google "POV porn." The website xHamster, subtitled its "POV Porn Videos" category as "Sex from Your Point of View," with the further description: "Naughty girls suck your dick and demand hard fucking in POV porn videos. Screw the sluts and cum all over them from your point of view at xHamster."

As already noted, technological advances in streaming platforms make pornography easier to see now than ever before. People can watch pornography on their laptops, tablets, and mobile phones as well as on hi-def home television systems. Consumers are also twice as likely to stream pornography through a handheld device than view it on a computer.[13] This means that people are watching porn in places that would have been unthinkable 30 years ago, like in a classroom, the workplace, or a *public* place. For example, during a layover in the Philadelphia airport in spring 2017 I grabbed a pretzel dog and paused in a small food alcove to quickly eat it before my next flight. A 30-ish-year-old white man sat down two tables over and began streaming porn that I could both hear and see. Semipublic porn viewing is also happening in strip clubs. Exotic dancers share that some customers are watching pornography on their phones after they pay a cover to see *live* naked women.[14]

Kayla believes that "men are constantly using their smartphones to look up porn." She explained that they watch porn, "not just at night, or on their computer, or a magazine. Porn is available all the time." Then, she shared a story:

> I remember I was in the process of moving with an ex-boyfriend and we were loading the truck. He had just gone to the bathroom. I went to look at his phone and he had porn on there in the middle of when we're loading the moving truck. I guess he had gone to the bathroom and was looking at porn before, during, or after he was taking a poo. I said, 'Well there's porn on your phone," and he was like, "Oh shit."

Among the people I interviewed, most believe that "all" men and "many" women watch internet porn, as Dylan, who is white and 28, explains: "Almost everyone I know watches it. I would say that a lot of women that are my age watch it and 100% of the men. Everyone down the line. It's an unspoken guy rule, everyone jacks off every day."[15]

Statistics that substantiate how many men and women view internet pornography are hard to generate, and vary widely. However, it is possible to track the demographics, behaviors, and preferences of users of a specific site like Pornhub, the largest pornography-sharing website on the internet. In 2018, 71% of Pornhub's users were male and 29% female. Consumers made 33.8 billion visits to Pornhub and viewed 207,405 videos per minute. Pornhub videos received 141,312,502 votes, more than the number cast in the 2016 US presidential election. The countries with the most overall traffic to Pornhub were the United States at number one, followed by the United Kingdom at two, and India at three. Globally, the six most popular searches were, in order: "lesbian," "hentai," "MILF," "stepmom," "Japanese," and "mom." Pornhub parses the data by country, age, gender, device, time spent per visit, even operating systems and web browsers.[16]

Gonzo Porn—Not 1970s-esque Sexy Plumber and Bored Housewife Plots

Contemporary pornography can be roughly separated into two categories: feature films and gonzo. Feature films mimic the conventions of regular movies with a plot and characters. Some, like the 2005 feature *Pirates XXX*, pornify a mainstream movie, in this case, *Pirates of the Caribbean: The Curse of the Black Pearl*. In contrast, gonzo porn, described as wall-to-wall sex scenes, has only the barest semblance of a plot (if that), a low budget, and promotes its content as "real." Because gonzo porn is much cheaper to make and produce than feature porn, that's most of what someone searching online for free porn will find. Tube technology in the mid-'00s hastened the creation and dissemination of free porn as sites like YouTube (created in 2005) permitted users to share content.[17] Researchers also began documenting an increasing amount of violence depicted in internet pornography at this time.[18] One of the more chilling moments recorded in the 2007 Media Education film *The Price of Pleasure* is an interview with a pornographer at the AVN Adult Entertainment Expo in Las Vegas who, when queried about the amount of violence in internet pornography, responded wryly, "The future of porn is violence."

Gonzo showcases sex acts that women in general do not enjoy—like facial abuse and anal sex[19]—and others that are bizarre and "body punishing"[20]—like double penetration. Double penetration is a sex act in which two men penetrate a woman at the same time, one in her vagina and one in her anus. "Double vag" and "double anal" refer to two penises entering one orifice or the other at the same time. Besides uncomfortably (or violently) stretching the physical limits of a woman's body, double penetration extends the number of people who usually have sex together. Most people have sex by themselves (masturbating), or with one other person, not two. Further, any double penetration means there are two men with their penises touching or very close to one another, an unusually homoerotic act in a culture that still demonizes male same-sex behavior.[21] Gonzo porn also systematically layers brutality into the performers' sex by repeatedly showing women able and eager to endure grueling physical acts—e.g., "naughty girls suck your dick and demand hard fucking"—while directing male actors to spew verbal abuse at women in the scenes. "Dirty slut, ugly whore, dumb bitch, nasty cunt" are phrases commonly said in gonzo pornography by male to female performers. "Screw the sluts and cum all over them" was the description of the xHamster POV website content seen on Google *before* one even clicked on the link.

Much feminist research and analysis on pornography focuses on the sexist representations of women as always-compliant sex dolls. Less is written about representations of men in pornography who often play the role of sadistic brute—violent, menacing, selfish, and abusive. The "Money Shot" episode from the documentary series *Hot Girls Wanted: Turned On* (2017) shows how producers create these problematic representations of men and masculinity. The episode profiles Jax, an African American male porn star. We see him at work, behind the scenes, doing an interracial porn scene with Kylie, a white woman. Jax seems sweet, sensitive, and good-natured throughout the episode, smiling easily, and behaving carefully and gently with Kylie when they work. Jax is much bigger and older than Kylie: he is large and muscled, and looks to be in his early to mid-30s, while Kylie is 18 years old and petite.

The viewer observes Jax become uncomfortable during a scene when the producers direct him to do faux violence to Kylie. He is repeatedly told to "choke her," and "smash her face, be rough with her," and to put his fingers in her mouth, pull it open, and make a "mean face." As far as one watching can tell, Kylie is not physically hurt, but she is posed in ways that mimic violence, and directed to assume expressions of fear. Meanwhile, Jax performs the character of a violent, dominating brute. The viewer learns in an aside that "Jax doesn't like to do rough scenes. He's a more passionate, romantic kind of guy." Regardless of Jax's or Kylie's preferences, the end result is in the hands of producers who create another derivative regurgitation of sexist and racist stereotypes dished up for those who want to masturbate to interracial porn in which a "black guy roughs up a white teen."

Student Porn Compilations

In 2013, five young women in my sex industry class decided to do their own content analysis and illustration of contemporary porn for their group project. They did a Google search of "porn" and "sex," and chose to feature videos from the first page of results. The students explained that they did not hunt down "the worst stuff"—torture porn and bukkake,[22] for example—but instead followed the lead of researchers examining the content of the *most viewed* pornography.[23] The final project featured video footage of eight clips of gonzo pornography interspersed with screen shots of still advertisements that they said "bombarded them repeatedly" while they worked on the compilation. We watched it the final week of the semester. The class knew one group had chosen to make a pornography compilation, and we had been curious what they would find and create. We expected it might be difficult to watch, but the compilation was even worse than we imagined.[24]

The collection of videos evidenced a stunning amount of violence against women. For example, one clip spotlighted a woman enduring "facial abuse." Also called "face fucking," facial abuse is pornography that features rough oral sex in which a male performer violently gags a woman with his penis while spitting on, slapping, and insulting her. The students shared that this particular video had been immensely popular, receiving over 200,000 likes. In another, a man anally penetrated a woman in an office while calling her ugly and a dog, telling her to "bark like a dog," which she immediately did. Each video had been uniquely demeaning to the actors, presenting the male performers as menacing, huge, and brutal, and the female actors as willing objects, aroused by abuse with the exception of a racist rape scene which featured six black men entering a house and forcefully raping a white woman.

In 2019, a group of students decided to update the compilation to observe what had changed in the past six years. Like their predecessors, they collected a series of seven vignettes culled from the most popularly viewed porn on the first page of Google results. Five of the videos focused on some facet of incest—for example a mother with a son, and a sister and brother together—and the other video clips featured group sex. In the final clip, one woman gave oral sex to a circle of men in what seemed to be a version of bukkake. This content supports Pornhub data and recent stories on the rapid growth of "fauxcest," a type of porn in which the performers pretend to be related, and "threesome" porn.[25] Of the most searched terms in 2018, three were incest-related. In the United States, the top five searches were, in order: "MILF," "ebony," "threesome," "stepmom," and "hentai." *Maxim, Cosmopolitan,* the *Daily Beast, Marie Claire, Yahoo,* and *Vice* have all reported on the rise of fauxcest. *Vice* writer Gareth May quotes Dan O'Connell, founder of Girlfriend Films, a company that produces popular incest-themed porn series. O'Connell explained consumer interest in fauxcest as "about pushing boundaries. . . . Producers of adult movies . . . leave the realm of conventional sex and depict the very outer edges of sexual behavior." In other words, internet pornography continues to draw in consumers and keep their attention with new, "edgy" material, which, in 2019, was incest.[26] So, since *more* people are watching porn *more often* than ever before, and watching it *younger*, and the content of the most viewed pornography continually seeks a new edge, how is this affecting people's sex lives?

Act Like a Porn Star in Bed

Many who participated in this study observed that internet pornography is influencing what people think is sexy, as well as how they have sex.[27] For example, Alexis, who is white and 20, said, "I think women feel the need to look and act like a porn star in bed and do all these things they see in pornography when, a lot of times, it isn't even the best way." She continued:

> Women get it in their head that they have to have violent sex for it to be pleasurable or for men to like them. Every woman I know, at least one of their partners has gone too far or made them uncomfortable, or wish they wouldn't be so rough. Especially choking and facial abuse. A lot of that comes directly from porn. Men see it and think, "That's hot, I'm going to try that in bed," and most everyday women don't really like that stuff.

Approximately half of the women I interviewed shared stories of men engaging, or asking to engage, in sex acts that seemed to come "directly from porn" including: men choking, gagging, spanking, spitting on, and slapping women, double penetration, anal sex, facial abuse, the male orgasming on a female body or her face, handcuffs, threesomes, and men asking female partners to call them "daddy."

Heather, who is white and 22, described two friends who recently broke up with new boyfriends because of "borderline physical assault" during sex involving acts taken from pornography. Heather explained that, before then, her friends hadn't paid much attention to the fact that their partners were watching porn: "It's just porn, you know," Heather repeated, mimicking a shrug. That changed when the boyfriend of one tried to penetrate her anally without obtaining consent, and the boyfriend of the other "gagged her when she was performing oral sex really aggressively." Abigail, who is white and 21, also shared that her last two partners asked her to do sex acts straight from porn. She said,

> Guys expect you to do certain things in bed that you don't really want to do, or even think sounds good, but they think that it's normal. Especially when I came out as pansexual, they expect me to do certain things. They'll ask me if I'm okay with threesomes even though that's not a thing that normal, monogamous people do. And I'm just like, "Why would my sexuality automatically put that out there for you?" Or they think that even if you don't want threesomes with another girl, they'll be like, "Well can another guy join in? And we can do like, double anal or double vaginal." I don't want anything near me that is going to in any way hurt me. I know that that's painful, like it has to be painful. I think that, for them, that's real sex. That's how real sex should be.

Tara, who is white and 19, said, "Porn gives guys the wrong impression and encourages almost a dominance, like the guys should be abusive and controlling. I used to have a boyfriend who, his goal from the beginning of when we started dating was to get me to do anal, and I think that had something to do with porn."

Older women also discussed the impact of internet pornography in their relationships. Julia, who is 46, talked about pornography in the context of Christian evangelical expectations of sexual behavior. Evangelical culture discourages women and men from having sex before marriage, and frames pornography use as sinful.[28] At the same time, religiosity rarely buffers one completely from mainstream culture. Julia observed that Christian men who have not had sex but watched a lot of pornography had unrealistic expectations of women. She said, "They get frustrated, 'What do you mean I have to work for 15 minutes to get you aroused? What do you mean you're not going to orgasm if I fuck you really hard? What do you mean you've got pubic hair?' It's [porn] an unrealistic portrayal of what men and women do during sex that poisons face-to-face intimacy." Lauren, who is white and 39, described how pornography complicated her sex life when she was dating a man ten years younger. Her story illustrates what may ensue when negotiating sexual kinks in the era of internet porn. She narrated:

> There was a point where I was a little bit into spanking, and figuring it out, and it was fun. At some point he and I had this disagreement. We were having a text conversation and making up. He was still sort of annoyed, and then we were playing with that dynamic a little bit. He said he wanted to spank me and I was fine, and then he brought it a step further. I said, "What else would you want?" and he said something about "fucking my mouth."
>
> When I see it on porn, I think that woman is gagging and her eyes are tearing up because she's gagging and it's not a comfortable thing. It was something I know he's seen. I was like, "You understand that that's actually a very uncomfortable thing for me, that's a very different dynamic than a consensual fun spanking, you making me gag just because of something you've seen and incorporated from your porn."
>
> He was ten years younger than me. I felt like I was constantly being like, "Okay, this actually doesn't work for me, like that's what this is." He got it, he did, he's a good person and understands, but he's a 30-year-old white man who watches porn. He's grown up with porn. He didn't have anything other than porn to masturbate to and watch, just hang out and watch, not even to masturbate. Just have it on, as entertainment.

Lauren demonstrates maturity and self-awareness about her own desires and boundaries, as well as insight about her partner's perspective, in this story. As Layna's story below illustrates, young women still learning who they are and what they like, and who want to please young men, may not yet have the tools to express themselves.

A Latinx and Pacific Islander 20-year-old woman, Layna described a friend's sexual assault that mimicked a porn scene. Her friend "Fran" had had a "threesome" with two football players at a frat party. Layna narrated, "Fran was so drunk and she went in a room with this one guy and started giving him oral. Then she said that this guy just came out of nowhere and started hitting it from the back, another guy." In other words, another fraternity member entered the room and penetrated Fran vaginally without any discussion of consent while she was giving oral sex to someone else. Layna explained, "She didn't show that she was upset about it, but she did show that it was like, 'What the fuck?' She didn't give them the okay to double-team her like that. It literally sounds like an episode in a porn thing." When I asked Layna why Fran didn't say, "Stop, get off me, who are you?" etc., Layna said, "She just continued and got out of there as soon as possible. She has that image of being a fun party girl."

How Do We Know What We Don't Know?

One argument people make in defense of pornography is that it is fantasy, and viewers are intelligent and sophisticated enough to *know* that most real women don't want to be "double-teamed," to be spit on, gagged, ordered to bark like a dog, and insulted during sex. But how do people "know" this? It's logical for viewers, especially young ones with no sexual experience or education, to think that women like porn sex. Contemplate some of the things you did not know when you were young, and learned the hard way. In my case, the first boy I ever kissed opened his mouth wide and slobbered all over me and that's what I thought kissing was until I learned otherwise.

Jordan's story here illustrates the problems inherent in expecting children to mysteriously "know" that most real people don't like porn sex, as well as issues related to easy access and the sexist content of internet porn. A white, 20-year-old bisexual woman, Jordan frankly described herself as a recovered "porn addict, who has been clean for the past two years."[29] Jordan's exposure to pornography started, she said, when she was 14 years old and "found a porn video." She explained that she didn't completely understand it at first, and had never masturbated before, but from watching porn she learned how to orgasm. I asked her if the pornography she saw was violent. She narrated:

> A lot of stuff was violent, yeah. I pretty much googled pornography and whatever popped up is what I saw. I knew I was addicted because it got to the point to where I had a set time: I would watch it for two hours every day. I was thinking about sex all the time and I realized I had a problem and I was like, "What is going on?" It really confused me. It totally messed me up on what I thought I liked or didn't like because I was a virgin until I was 19. I didn't really do anything sexual until I was in college. Then my first boyfriend I had, we wouldn't even have sex, but we would just be making out and he's very rough. It got to the point where he was biting me. I had bruises on me.
>
> He hurt me, and in my head I was thinking, "Well this is what it's supposed to be like," because you always have the image of the big, strong guy manhandling this chick on porn. And I'm like, "Oh well, everyone fantasizes about a big, strong guy, this is what I'm supposed to like." But it got to the point where I got out of the dorm showers, and one day this girl saw the bite marks and bruises on my shoulders and stuff, and she literally stopped and looked surprised, and kind of grossed out and kept walking and I was like, "Okay, so this isn't normal, this isn't okay."
>
> I stopped seeing that person, he had anger issues. I'm just curious if I had never been a porn addict at such a young age would I have been in certain situations like the guy who would literally leave bruises on me? I was thinking, "I guess this is what people want, this rough stuff," and it was awful. I hated it. I never felt pleasure from it. I feel like I would have been less confused with what I enjoyed sexually if I hadn't watched it, I guess. It's definitely not, a lot of it, is not made to pleasure women.

Most pornography consumers have to have at least one time of trying a porn sex act out, and having it go badly (or well), to understand what pleases them. Even then, as Jordan's story shows, they might think that the pornographers know better than they do. Early exposure to internet pornography impeded Jordan's ability to set boundaries, made her vulnerable to sexual abuse, and obscured her inner sexual guidance.

Hookup Sex and Porn

Several women, like Faye and Rebecca, told stories about porn sex in the context of a hookup. Researchers find that relationship sex is more equitable in terms of mutual orgasms and overall enjoyment for women than hookup sex.[30] Hooking up includes any type of sexual interaction without the expectation of romantic intimacy or commitment.[31] Hookups usually last no longer than an evening, and sometimes no more than a few minutes. Some speculate that hookup culture, which involves much alcohol, ritualized grinding on a dance floor, and little conversation, is replacing dating for young people.[32] Faye, white and 26, was visibly upset as she described a man spitting on her during a hookup. She said:

> I was so ashamed that I told very few people. I stopped him and was like, "That's not cool, I'm not okay with this," and he was like, 'I just thought this was going to make the situation better for you. I'm trying anything I can to turn you on," and I said, "The fact that your brain even went to spitting on me is awful, like no. That's something you should ask someone before you do it, or wait for them to tell you that that's what they want you to do." I could tell by the way he was having sex that he watched a lot of porn. I think that's something he grabbed from that, and was like, "Oh let's do this." After that happened, I was kind of fucked up from it. I was like, "I've never been spat on or anything." I've never felt so disrespected in my life.

Rebecca, who is white and 25, described a bad sexual experience she had with a man she met at a bar. Her plan was to "get out there and have sex with someone," to deliberately try out hooking up. Rebecca felt attracted to the potential hookup, thought he was cute, and figured this was her chance to be adventurous. When her "fun hookup" was unexpectedly rough during sex, Rebecca said she felt confused, and became paralyzed and powerless. Rebecca shared, "I felt weird at the time. I didn't want to do it, but I was shocked. He slapped and spanked me, and I felt very much like an object, not even a person, a plaything. I remember I felt gross the next day. I was this passive participant that was just sort of thrown around however he wanted." Never having experienced being treated like this, or imagining that someone would do so uninvited, Rebecca had no plan in place for how to handle it. Like many young women, she blamed herself for going home with a stranger, for being unprepared, and for not speaking out at the time.[33] Rebecca's response—freezing up—is likely an illustration of "tonic immobility," a "temporary state of motor inhibition in response to situations involving intense fear," a state described by many rape victims.[34]

Male Sexual Dysfunction

In addition to discussing porn sex influencing acts introduced face-to-face, participants also noted other troubling consequences of internet pornography: some men and women are struggling with watching too much of it, and some men are experiencing difficulties climaxing without porn.[35] Kayla, who is 28, said frankly, "My age is really when men started having very easy access to porn through the internet and you can see the damage." Kayla shared that two of the four men she's been with sexually "had significant trouble climaxing." She attributed this to pornography, saying, "I think that they have used porn so frequently to masturbate, or get turned on and orgasm that, in a situation with a real woman who is not just there to be their porn fantasy, then they have trouble." Kayla believes that "porn and video games have destroyed an entire generation of men." She explained:

> I have noticed that it's really hard for them [men] to find satisfaction from having sex without doing something nontraditional. The stereotype used

to be, "Oh you know men can have sex with anything and enjoy it," but now it's like they want to ejaculate in your face, or they need to have anal sex, or they need to put their hand around your throat. There is always something. Even the most normal seeming people want to try something like that, and if you're like "no," then you're the weird one, because it's like everyone has a fetish, everyone does something.

Andrew, who is white and 24, connected his overuse of pornography as a boy to erectile issues in his sexual relationships. He said,

From age 13 and onward it was just me being given free domain over what I wanted to do. I was home alone most of the time and that was when it started [watching a lot of porn]. I'm desensitized to actual sex. I'm unable to finish during normal sex and it's not because there's something missing from it. There's so much sexual stimulus outside of sex that when actual sex comes into play. . . . I've quit using porn as much and I think that's helped.

Andrew believes that his early and frequent porn use affects how he perceives and responds to the quality of stimulation with a partner, ultimately inhibiting his ability to climax. Abigail confided that both of her last two boyfriends had difficulties "finishing because they weren't looking at porn. Right now with the relationship I'm in, we're working on it and trying to figure out how to satisfy him better without having to use that, but it's hard. [He had been looking at it for ten years.] He started looking at it when he was ten years old." Abigail also discussed a friend who regulates his porn use in order to orgasm with his girlfriend. She said, "He has to stop watching porn and masturbating three to four weeks in advance before he has sex with his girlfriend because he can't finish unless he completely stops and rids himself of it for a while." Abigail summed up the thoughts of many participants:

It's become much harder to have sex with a man who is obsessed or addicted to porn because real sex doesn't compare to what he sees on the screen. It's harder for men to want real women. As a result, it makes having real sex harder because they aren't turned on, or they can't get off, and it makes me and other women, too, probably, feel inadequate. It reinforces the idea that women aren't good enough and lowers our self-esteem, which can contribute to eating disorders and unnecessary plastic surgery and all kinds of things. I'm a sex-radical feminist, but even I agree that this level of obsession with porn has pretty much destroyed our sex lives.

While the people I interviewed focused on problems associated with pornography, social science data examining the effects of pornography use in consumers' lives tell a varied story. For example, in one survey of 430 people "no negative effects" was the most commonly noted consequence of pornography use in their relationships.[36] In contrast, another study of 308 college women found that "their male partner's frequency of pornography use were negatively associated with their relationship quality . . . and negatively correlated with self-esteem, relationship quality, and sexual satisfaction."[37] In general, studies tend to find that porn use has a negative effect in relationships and may cause personal distress, *and* that some feel positively about pornography to the degree that it increases sexual knowledge and reduces sexual puritanism. The fact is that viewers can find new information that enhances their sex lives *and* be bombarded with sexist representations of women and men in internet pornography.[38]

Pushing the Envelope

In my interviews the word "desensitized" emerged 50% of the time when discussing both raunch culture and internet pornography. For example, Andrew observed, "I've noticed within the last five or six years as porn is much more easily accessible than it used to be, it's sort of a desensitization, like they need something more than they could find in the past for the same thing." Andrew shares a house with four other young men and said that they watch a lot of porn. He noticed that his roommates are watching more and more "intense" content in order to achieve a climax. Andrew clarified, "In the past when I was a teenager, the fact that you could find porn at all was like, 'Oh wow, I found a picture of a naked person!' But now it's people getting into progressively more, I don't know what the exact word would be, intense things." I inquired what exactly "intense" referred to and Andrew responded, "Well, multiple, 15-guy gang bang stuff and they would be like, 'Oh wow, that was really intense! Let's see if I can find something that's even more.' And they'll just keep looking for bigger deals. It's almost like a badge of, 'Oh look how cool I am.'" He observed that the more women are degraded in porn, "the more people view it."

As internet porn grows more "edgy," so does mainstream programming. I argue that the content of internet porn is *driving* popular culture. Western media depicts much sexualized violence, and violence period, in broadcast television (*American Horror Story, Lucifer, Sons of Anarchy, Law & Order: Special Victims Unit, Blood Drive*), cable and streaming TV (*Westworld, Game of Thrones, The Americans, House of*

FIGURE 2.1. Gigi and Bella Hadid on the cover of British *Vogue*, March 2018. Source: *Vogue*

FIGURE 2.2. Advertisement for torture porn website.
Source: Punishtube.com

Cards, Ray Donovan, Thirteen Reasons Why, Shameless), films (*Suicide Squad, The Hills Have Eyes, Piranha, Mother*), and music videos (Maroon 5, "Animals"; Rihanna, "Bitch Better Have My Money"). Further, most contemporary R-rated or unrated movies now also include graphic nudity, soft-core pornography, and/or crude humor relating to sexuality. Further, after news outlets began reporting on the rise of fauxcest porn in 2015,[39] images suggesting fauxcest began to appear in mainstream media. For example, the 2019 television series *Almost Family* portrayed an accidental incest scene in the pilot episode. Consider also the March 2018 cover of British *Vogue* featuring sisters Gigi and Bella Hadid (see figure 2.1).

Andrew described one of his friends who he said was "weirded out" that he "can't get off to the same things anymore." Pornography researchers confirm Andrew's observations: seeing the same type of image repeatedly ceases to sexually stimulate the viewer.[40] To reiterate, image producers seek a new edge to attract consumers, and sometimes that edge is an amoral, misogynist, sexualized violence as seen in figure 2.2, which features a torture porn still.

So why has the content of internet pornography evolved toward violence and bizarre sex acts? Psychologist R. Douglas Fields highlights research that finds a biological connection in the brain between violence and arousal, describing it as a "nasty legacy of our primate ancestors."[41] Culturally, while rates of global violence may be at a historic low,[42] media violence has increased in quantity, and become "more graphic, sexual, and sadistic."[43] Violence shocks people, and gets their attention, and with attention follows subscriptions and money. In a capitalist society, linking sex and violence in pornography and then walking viewers into more and more extreme content is likely the quickest, and least costly, way to make a profit.

Talking about Pornography—Who Is the "Nasty Whore"?

As I hope is well illustrated in this chapter, internet pornography is a new phenomenon characterized not just by sexist content, but by violent sexist content and previously taboo acts like incest. Most gonzo pornography centers male pleasure while showing men insulting women and roughly penetrating women's bodies. Instead of ignoring this content, let's think about it. What does it mean that the words one can easily find in pornography demean women: "dumb slut," "stupid bitch," "nasty whore"? What do you think about the fact that men are making sexual content for other men which entails hiring and directing porn performers to paint women as dirty, sex-crazed, promiscuous, and inferior in order to turn the biggest profit? If anyone could be rightfully dubbed the "nasty whore" in this equation, it's the pornographers, not the female performers. At the same time, I don't think there is a malevolent cadre of male supremacists actively conspiring to oppress and abuse women. I think the pornographers are simply following the money. This is an illustration of the technological revolution creating unanticipated consequences: as the porn engine drives the tech engine, representations of human sexuality suffer.

It's not that "dirty talk" is necessarily oppressive. The problem is that watchers see mind-numbing clip after clip of men calling women sluts, bitches, whores, and dogs absent any context in gonzo porn. This gives some viewers, especially young ones, the impression that half of all men secretly want to harangue women as they have sex, to slap a female partner, and call her names while pounding away. I think it's important to have open and frank conversations with significant others, children, teens, and students about this content and what it means. I know this is hard to do. People, in general, have little practice discussing sex, *especially* the new acts featured in pornography: misogynist insults to women, gang bangs, facial abuse, double penetration, and fauxcest. Also, most Westerners consider sexual desires private, and porn use is a (mostly) private act. Moreover, internet porn also suffers from a condition of inarticulation—we don't know how to talk about it. Consider Andrew's use of the word "intense" to describe his roommates watching increasingly extreme pornography. Interview subjects also described violent pornography as "crazy shit" and "weird." These gender neutral, vague words mask the inequality of internet pornography, the fact that it is *sexist*. The "15-guy gang bang" that Andrew mentioned earlier refers to 15 men penetrating one woman.

Making matters even grimmer, US citizens do not well understand how structures shape us. Marinating in individualism our whole lives, we are trained to perceive social life as a consequence of individual choices and actions. Thus, people often mistake a structural critique of the sexism and racism in pornography as a personal attack on their individual desires and preferences, and some respond defensively. Finally, pornography is a product of patriarchy and patriarchy supplies its citizens with a *wealth* of language to perpetuate its dominance. It may be hard to talk about fauxcest, facial abuse, or the strange sexualization of hamburgers in a Hardee's commercial, but phrases that silence critiques of pornography and pornification spring easily to the lips: "You don't like porn, what are you, a prude? Maybe you just need to look harder. You're not a feminazi, are you? You must just hate sex. Are you advocating for censorship? We have to protect the First Amendment. You need to loosen up and get laid. Stop trying to regulate my sex life. You must be really repressed."

Kayla explained that when she critiques pornography, or sexist elements of popular culture, she is dismissed as "repressed" and too "politically correct." Kayla shared:

> Being politically correct is also seen as shrill, shrewish, controlling and uptight. "Oh you don't have to be so PC about everything." If you don't think rape jokes are funny, or pedophile jokes are funny, or whatever, then you're uptight. Then people jump to this, "Oh America is so repressed in our sexuality. We need to be like European countries." And I think you're taking the wrong lessons from that because, I'm sure raunch culture is a thing over there too because we're in a global society, but not being repressed does not mean you watch porn all the time on your phone and can't have a real sexual relationship with a real person. That's not what lack of repression means. Lack of repression means that we have better sex education, that we don't feel guilty for having sex before you're married, that we make people learn what consent means, that we make people learn how to have safe sex, that we give people access to contraception; that's what lack of sexual repression looks like, not "I get to watch whatever kind of porn I want whenever I want, and you have to be okay with it or you're a prude."

Silencing people who critique pornography by calling them prudish or repressed is a patriarchal illustration of doublespeak because most internet pornography itself *illustrates* repression by relentlessly casting men as selfish sadists plundering female bodies while rendering irrelevant female desire and pleasure. Studies show that millennials, the group that watches the most internet pornography, report having less sex than Baby Boomers and Generation Xers did at the same age.[44] I speculate that internet pornography and raunch culture play an important role in this. If all I knew about sex was gonzo pornography, I would be scared to have it.

Internet pornography has some serious drawbacks. I consider most of it sexist and silly, sexist and disturbing, or just sexist. However, I believe it's valuable to keep one's sex life spiced up, and add new acts to one's sexual repertoire. I support people exploring their desires consensually however they manifest. To do so, I find it valuable to distinguish pornography (to me, a patriarchal product) from erotica. Erotica encompasses both words and images. It situates arousal in the context of a story, a reason *why* people are having sex, and features mutual pleasure. I also advocate a robust, pleasure-centered sex education curriculum in public schools, and a culture of conversation about sexuality and pornography. Not "Ha ha, better sanitize the keyboard before you touch it," nor "Ooh, gross, I don't want to hear about my parents having sex," nor "Better stay a virgin until marriage," nor "Dude, I banged the hottest chick last night," but meaningful dialogue about love, connection, desire, and pleasure.

3

"Be the Man That Treats Her Like a Lady, but Still Grabs Her Ass"

In 2018, of the 7.2 billion humans living on planet Earth, 3.03 billion actively used social media. Launched over the preceding decade and a half, Facebook (2004), Instagram (2010), Reddit (2005), Snapchat (2011), Tinder (2012), Twitter (2006), Tumblr (2007), Vine (2013), WhatsApp (2009), YouTube (2005), and many other platforms have transformed social life. Facebook is the most popular with 2.072 billion users while Instagram is the fastest growing with 800 million monthly consumers.[1] The 20-somethings I interviewed discussed Instagram, Snapchat (300 million users), Tinder (25 million users),[2] and Facebook the most often, with Instagram the clear platform of choice among them. Both Instagram and Snapchat are widely used by youth: 90% of Instagram and 70% of Snapchat users are under 34.[3] Finally, 90% of people aged 18–29 use social media compared to 35% of those over 65.[4] Smartphones allow people to access this stream of social media anywhere at any time. Indeed, a recent survey finds that the average internet user spends 142 minutes a day on social media.[5] Millennials often discussed seeing raunch culture on their favorite platforms. They said: "You have to write about social media!" "Instagram is where people flaunt themselves," "Snapchat is a huge thing," "I get upset if I don't get more than 200 likes," "People live a life so they can put it on social media," "These women I see on Instagram, are they bots or are they real?"

With so many people now interacting digitally, and more predicted to do so each passing month, scholars are analyzing how screen-mediated communications shape us.[6] Sociologist Sherry Turkle, for example, explores how social media puts users into a "Facebook zone," similar to the "machine zone" reported by slot machine gamblers and video gamers, a

FIGURE 3.1. Example of sexist meme.
Source: memegenerator.net

state of hypnotized play. In the Facebook zone, consumers compulsively scroll never-ending new content, switching from app to app, finding it a struggle to close all the apps and put down the device. Turkle describes the experience of a young user, how the "process of checking draws her into the process of checking," who doesn't close the app, but, at the same time, does not make a conscious decision to continue scrolling.[7] Perhaps some reading this have opened Facebook or Twitter or Instagram during a free moment only to find, after finally dragging one's attention from the screen, that 30 minutes, an hour, or more has evaporated. People linger in social media sites because the technology is *designed* to encourage users to do so.[8] I want to take a closer look at the environment in which young people most often see raunch culture: the strange new world of social media. Here, I explore how it affects consumers to scroll through a limitless feed of sexist memes (see figure 3.1 for an example) and provocative selfies for hours a day.

"Not Good Enough"

In 2017, 81% of Americans owned smartphones, spending, on average, four hours a day on them.[9] We use our phones for work, entertainment, socializing, news, and shopping. Studies show that every generation is spending more time on their phones each passing year and, in what is

FIGURE 3.2. Screenshot of Kim Kardashian demonstrating waist training.
Source: Kim Kardashian

FIGURE 3.3. Photo of Charlotte McKinney.
Source: PageSix.com

sure to be a surprise to precisely no one, young people are the heaviest users. For example, Makenzie, who is white and 19, shared that the first thing she does in the morning, after rolling over and turning off the alarm on her phone, is to "see who has texted me and what kind of notifications I have. If I have time, I'll get on social media and check to see if anyone has messaged me." Thus, before Makenzie even leaves her bed many mornings, she'll see some provocative selfies, perhaps a story about a celebrity revealing her side boob or doing "waist training," sexy advertisements, and #goals posts of impossibly thin and attractive couples (gay and straight).

According to those I interviewed, their social media feeds—a hodge-podge of friends' and followers' posts, porn bots, and sponsored and targeted ads—raise feelings of envy, jealousy, and insecurity. In her 2017 book *The Happiness Effect*, researcher Donna Freitas found that social media is making young people depressed. This is because social media facilitates *comparisons*, a key source of unhappiness in humans. Comparisons come naturally to us; they are how we measure our successes

FIGURE 3.4. Social media influencers Kelly + Kody. Source: Instagram

and failures. We automatically and effortlessly compare our jobs, cars, mates, vacations, children, and bodies with others and, when we find ourselves lacking, an inevitability given we cannot be the best, smartest, most accomplished and attractive people *all the time*, we feel bad.[10] Just as internet pornography allows viewers to see historically unprecedented numbers of different women, social media enables widespread destructive comparisons simply not possible a short 25 years ago. It's not that people weren't despondent and unsatisfied when comparing themselves with others in earlier eras but that the cultural acceleration of print and television media followed by the internet, and now social media, offers new and more numerous ways to compare oneself to others.

Further, most present an idealized self[11] on social media. We curate our profiles to feature our most flattering photos, impressive accomplishments, and fun times.[12] Donna Freitas described social media as a place where users feel a "*duty* to appear happy." *Appearing* happy is obviously not the same as *feeling* happy. Indeed, investing time and energy in the very qualities that social media promotes—appearance, status, and image—*lowers* measurable happiness.[13] Perhaps some reading this have felt insecure, anxious, and the FOMO (fear of missing out) when scrolling through your feed. This is because even when we *know* that our "friends'" photos are carefully selected and possibly enhanced with apps to slim a face or brighten skin, and that the raucous time folks *seem* to be having might be enhanced for the camera, we still compare ourselves and feel lacking. For example, I recently went to a birthday party that started out tense and stressful, and got worse after one of the people attending revealed upsetting information. It was a relief to leave the event. Later I saw a picture of the cake and balloons from the party on social media and actually thought, "Oh that looks fun, I wish I had been there," banging my head a moment later realizing I *had* been there and it had been horrible. The idealized version was so different than the actual experience I did not recognize it at first. Sharing the most flattering pieces of our experiences absent the context distorts our perceptions of fun, happiness, success, love, and friendship. This is partly why those who take "Facebook fasts," unplugging themselves from social media for a period of time, report improved well-being.[14]

But, while we know our own posts are performances at least part of the time, we still feel inadequate when we scroll through other people's feeds. Courtney, who is white and 20, described an entire generation of young people feeling like they are "not good enough" because of social media. Courtney said, "If they had nothing to compare themselves to, then they would be good enough. Because you can't help but see that they're attractive and you're like, 'Well, why don't I look like that? Why don't me and my girlfriend take cute pictures like that? Why aren't we both stick thin?'" Like Courtney, Cecilia, who is white and 25, explained that social media puts a lot of pressure on young people to look a certain way, have a glamorous life, and own the latest high-status item:

> Because we're able to see people from all over the world, I think it puts more pressure. You see people traveling and you're like, "Why am I not travelling? I'm not well-travelled yet," or all these women I see on Instagram, "Are they bots or are they real?" They give me terrible self-esteem. Everyone is always on their phones. It's comparison all the time. You think, *Oh my gosh, they're doing so much with their life, how are they doing that? I'm older than they are, how are they going and doing something with their lives? How can they look like that? How can they afford all that?* I think it really makes materialistic things very important to how we are, and people put a lot of pressure on that.

Those I interviewed described comparing their bodies, the number of likes they received, their relationships, their belongings, their friendships, their vacations, and their social lives on social media.

Beyond the in person comparisons evaluating who has the newest designer jeans, the latest hair fashion, or gets the best grade on a quiz, social media users learn about the goings-on of an ever-widening network of friends of friends. This creates insecurity, like Cecilia just described, as well as other unexpected consequences. For example, romantic breakups and friendship-endings may be harder to put behind you if you continue to see the old boyfriend who cheated on you, or the best friend who stopped talking to you for no clear reason, on social media. Even if you delete or un-follow the once close intimate, you will likely see them in *other* people's feeds. Features that allow all users to see who likes what can also create conflicts: *Why does "Taylor" always get more likes on her photos than I do?* Or, *Who is my partner messaging on social media?* Or, *Why did my boyfriend like a picture of some random woman (or his old girlfriend) in a bikini?* Cecilia elaborated:

> Social media makes people so paranoid and insecure because you can sometimes see what photos people have liked. So if you are, for example, a young woman and you are in a relationship and you see your boyfriend like these pictures of women that pose half-naked or they're in bikinis or they're in lingerie and they have the "perfect body," then you automatically are like, "Oh my gosh, I need to look like that because I need to please him." I think it adds a lot of pressure to be like, "Well I need to be perfect for my boyfriend."

It can also compromise trust between partners and friends. Cecilia shared that one of her friends deleted her Instagram account after she got engaged. Makenzie explained that many of her peers hesitate to post a new relationship status on social media for fear that others might "prey" on the new love. In some cases, opportunities to mistrust and resent "friends" are built into the design of a social media platform. For example, although Snapchat has since changed this feature, when it first launched it ranked a user's top three "best friends," according to a "magical friendship algorithm" that counted the number of snaps two people exchange.[15] Makenzie explained some of the tension this feature created:

> I remember when Snapchat first came out you could see everyone's top three best friends. That created a huge problem for people because when you send snaps they disappear. So girls would be insecure if Jennifer was

on their boyfriend's top friends, or vice versa. As far back as Myspace even, you could pick top friends. You could say I want a hundred top friends or three top friends. I remember when I had a Myspace back in fifth grade. Girls would get so excited when the boy that they liked put them as their top friend.[16]

I don't think Snapchat creators deliberately wanted to upset friend groups with the "best friends" element any more than Twitter employees wanted Tay, a learning AI I discuss in a later chapter, to spout neo-Nazi speech. Both are consequences of a culture in which the technologies we use to communicate with one another, as well as absorb and dispense information, are evolving more quickly than most of us can process. As journalist Thomas Friedman observes, humans are in a period of "exponential" technological growth.[17] And, as we begin to see and eliminate negative consequences of social media technology, new platforms emerge with new issues.

Context Collapse

Any reader with a social media account has probably experienced one of these new issues, "context collapse," and the accompanying tensions that occur when incompatible audiences read and respond to a post.[18] Face-to-face we share thoughts, feelings, and news depending upon who we are with and what we hope to accomplish: make friendly chitchat, work through an upsetting personal issue, vent about a work conflict, and/or express distress about a political event. However, when we say "what's on our mind" on a social media platform it reaches "friends" we know in *different* and *incompatible* contexts: elementary school, work, neighbors, relatives, teachers, passing acquaintances, students, friends of friends, and community leaders. Unless we create special groups of friends, itself a time-consuming and technologically demanding process requiring frequent updating, everyone in our circle may read a particular post.

Thus, in context collapse, not only do one's best girlfriends see a sexy selfie, so do one's grandmother and youth pastor. Expressing a political opinion that all one's college friends hold upsets a second cousin who responds vociferously angering a number of others. Sometimes we may simply learn things we really wish we didn't know such as "Jenny had a big party and invited everyone I know except me," or, "Uncle Bud is a climate change denier," or, "My grandfather thinks all the women coming forward to say #metoo are liars and sluts," or, "My ex is dating someone thinner than me."[19] I think often about Makenzie, Cecilia, and other young people managing relationships through the noise of social media. It's challenging enough to establish meaningful connections without the confusion of context collapse, the added stress of the unsolicited information found on social media, the opportunities for comparisons, and the barrage of sexist memes and sexy photos. Photo culture exacerbates all these issues.

Photo Culture

While it is nice to have a picture to remember an experience, photo culture—a term I am coining here that describes the social expectation born of the capacities of the smartphone to document and share our lives in all their daily detail in photos and videos—has many drawbacks. To begin with, the likelihood of picture-taking pressures many into putting more effort into their appearance before an event than they might otherwise—hair and makeup must be selfie-ready even for pizza and Netflix with friends. Cecilia observed, "It used to be you would have to call your friend up, and you would have to meet up to go hang out and stuff. But nowadays, when you do things with your friends, you dress up, you always take pictures, and it didn't used to be like that." Preparing for potential pictures is not only time-consuming, it also keeps a woman focused on her appearance, and beauty scholars note that any attention paid to looks usually has negative psychological consequences: the more conscious a woman is of her face and body, the more likely she is to dwell on elements of her physical self that displease her.[20]

Kayla observed that women "obsess over trying to get a picture where they look really good." She also felt that the possibility of measuring one's attractiveness against a river of others on social media fuels beauty obsessions:

> Women looking at other women's Facebook who they think are really attractive, or more attractive, or better, gives them an outlet to obsess even more: "Oh she's such a skinny bitch, why am I not?" They can't even go home and turn it off because they just get on Facebook. It's on constantly. It allows the competition to go everywhere with you, because it's in your phone, it's on your computer, that kind of thing.

Unflattering photos also create much anxiety. Laura, who is white, 32, and a therapist, shared that social media photos often come up in counseling sessions with teenagers: "They say, 'Can you believe what a revealing photo she's showing' and 'Here's all the things that people said about me in my bathing suit at the beach' and 'I can't believe my friend who went to the beach with me posted this picture, because I don't look hot in this picture.'" Laura elaborated, "It becomes this whole circle of, you can't even take pictures of yourself from that time you had at the beach, you have to choose very carefully what those pictures look like." Between happiness-killing comparisons, unwanted information, and anxiety about how one looks in one's own and friends' posts, it is not surprising that a number of studies published in the last ten years find that social media use negatively impacts people's self-esteem.[21]

To Objectify Is to Be the "Right Kind of Sexy"

Objectification theory, a framework for understanding how girls and women feel "looked-at," evaluates the mental health problems women risk negotiating a culture that objectifies female bodies. These include habitual body monitoring, depression, eating disorders, sexual dysfunction, shame, and anxiety.[22] Abigail, who is white and 21, illustrated some of the consequences of objectification when she said, "I know a lot of women now that aren't happy with their bodies. Even my friends, they can point to one thing that they like, but the rest of it they just don't like at all. And especially for me, I can't even point out one thing I like about myself." I inquired, "Just about your physical self and not your intelligence?" She sighed and said, "I can talk all day about how smart I am and how motivated I am and how hard-working I am, and I like my personality. I just don't like my physical self. But that takes over, 80 percent of what I think about, when I think about me. I don't even think about how smart I am. I just think about what I look like."

Teresa, who is 21 and Latinx, also shared that she struggles with body image issues because of raunch culture. She said:

> All the people I see are super skinny and have really blue eyes and even-toned skin (and I have five different tans going on at the moment), and super perfectly straight hair or nice controllable, wavy hair. It's an impossible image. I like food and I like the skin I have and I like the hair I have, but I do struggle with that because, I see that every day: these skinny, beautiful women are so desirable and I'm so undesirable.

Teresa succinctly described raunch culture as a "disease" and a "mistake that needs to be cleansed." She continued, "I don't like it. I feel as though it's very harmful to both men and women and it needs to stop immediately." Smartphone technology has also made it easy for users to photograph people in every imaginable place or situation, sometimes without their permission or knowledge. Timothy, who is white and 25, observed, "I see that with women they're constantly being afraid of being objectified. Because you don't know who is taking a picture of you on Snapchat if you walk down campus in leggings, you don't know if someone is behind you and Snapchatting your butt to his friends."

Kayla observed that raunch culture continues to narrow the range of ways women can perform the *right* kind of sexy. She explained:

> There is also this element that now you can't just be sexy, like Kim Kardashian traditional sexy, "Oh I'm wearing a really tight dress and heels." No, no, because then it's like, "She's obnoxious and high-maintenance." So you have to be a really specific type of sexy: you have to wear a men's shirt that's been washed so many times it's kind of see-through, and it's a little bit big, and comes down on your shoulder, and you're wearing it with cutoff shorts that are so short you can see your butt basically. You can't just look traditionally sexy, because then you just look like "a sorority bitch." You have to look, "Oh I didn't even try," but I'm still wearing this really skimpy whatever so I can simultaneously be sexy, *and* one of the guys *and* not care.

In social media, consumers compare their ability to look "effortlessly" sexy against that of celebrities, those who are "Instagram famous," friends, bots, and even idealized versions of themselves.

Since the paradigm of raunch makes compulsory sexy *self*-display, another consequence of photo culture is self-objectification. In other words, raunch culture acclimates viewers to a parade of airbrushed, almost naked female bodies, while smartphone technology allows girls and women to model *themselves* under the male gaze in sexy selfies. Making matters even more stressful, young people feel social pressure to "brand" themselves,[23] as Layna, who is Latinx/Pacific Islander and 20, fretted: "Everyone says that on Instagram you have, like, a style. So on Instagram people fight to have their own style, their own look on their pages. That's one thing I look at online and I feel like I don't have a theme." The Instagram selfie ideal that young women like Layna measure themselves against (see figure 3.5 for an example) is a personally branded reproduction of the male gaze on one's own body to *appear* naturally sexy and beautiful to one's followers (which may take 70 tries).

FIGURE 3.5. Alexis Ren, Instagram celebrity. Source: Instagram

Sexy Photos

Girls and women post sexy photos for the simple reason that these get the most positive feedback. Such photos combine all the stress and insecurity of beauty culture with the pornified dictates of raunch. It goes like this: people share their lives with followers through posted photos on a platform like Instagram. Some users value having many followers/friends, and most value a high percentage of "likes" on photos and posts relative to one's overall number of followers or friends because likes indicate attention and approval, give users a dopamine burst, and are a concrete measure of one's popularity.[24] For example, Elizabeth, who is white and 20, has 1,413 Instagram followers. She selectively posts one photo a day on her Instagram account with the goal of getting over 200 likes. Elizabeth said, "I get upset if I don't get more than 200. It won't ruin my whole day, but it kind of sucks and you try harder to get a better one next time." She described it as a "confidence boost" and a "goal—once I get this many, then I'll be fine," musing, "I think it's a part of society."

Laura said, "I spend a great deal of my time with teenagers talking about what's happening on social media and what people are doing, and if they're liking things or not liking things." She estimated that 25% of her session time with teenagers explores issues connected to social media. In addition to working through the problems social media creates in friendships, body image, jealousy, and self-esteem, Laura worried that social media also lowered users' internal reserves. She said, "I think raunch culture and social media have made it to where we receive so much external reinforcement we don't know how to provide our own internal reinforcement or intrinsic reinforcement for goals we set for ourselves." Several people I interviewed said that it is common for people to take down photos that don't receive a perceived adequate number of likes. Cecilia shared that some of her friends strategically post at specific times of the day known to have high traffic but low postings in order to increase potential likes. It doesn't take a young woman long to learn that sexier photos get more likes, chili peppers (emojis that convey one is hot), and complimentary comments such as "Gorgeous body!" Figure 3.6 illustrates the point.

Elizabeth is well aware of which types of photos get the most positive feedback:

> When I post a picture I know what will get more likes. If I'm just doing one of me, or one with my friends, cause we're in a sorority and it's a cute picture talking about how happy we are with our friends, people aren't as likely to like that. If it's a picture of me and my friends going out with a

FIGURE 3.6A-B. Instagram post with comments. Source: Instagram

little more makeup on and dressed, not even scantily clad, it's just more hot versus cute. Try to be more hot than pretty. And then you have other women commenting, "Hot," and they'll use the little fire emoji which means you look really hot.

Rebecca, who is white and 25, observed this as well:

On Instagram, there are women who have accounts and if they're really beautiful they get lots of followers and they get lots of likes, particularly if they show a lot of skin and they get a lot of attention that they probably think is positive. I had a cousin who takes a lot of selfies on Facebook, and she gets a lot of likes from that, and she feels good about herself because people like her photos. She might make a kissy-face or something.

Brian, white and 25, follows 82 people on Instagram and knows a little over half of them. The others he "noticed." He shared that he follows women he does not know on Instagram simply *because* they post "hot" pictures. During our interview, he pulled up his account to show me. Brian's feed included photo after photo of women posing provocatively, many with breast and butt cleavage prominently displayed. A full 75% of his content was women posting sexy selfies. I asked him if he considered Instagram an alternate form of pornography, and if he ever got bored with these kinds of pictures. He responded:

> I never get tired of seeing them, but at the same time that's all Instagram is. It's just girls taking selfies and pictures with friends. Guys have Instagrams too, but if you look at girls on Instagram and guys on there, there's a clear difference. I'd say most of a girl's feed is them in their bikinis, and even if they're clothed trying to show their cleavage off. You can read all the comments from people who don't even know that person saying, "Wow, you're really hot" or "You have nice tits."

Evidence of androsexism also emerged in Brian's description of Instagram comments. Echoing what Elizabeth shared, Brian said that girls and women frequently compliment *other* women's bodies.[25] But, he continued, "just because a girl makes a comment like that, nobody assumes she's a lesbian. Even if she does, I guess guys like lesbians too where even if they knew you were a lesbian, and were attracted to you, they would probably still try to pursue you." Evidence of the "stalled revolution"[26]—in which it is more culturally accepted for women to be like men than men to be like women—there is simply no parallel of heterosexual men appreciating one another's bodies, of commenting, "nice abs," "biceps," or "butt" on a man's photo. If that happened, Brian speculated, "Guys [would] get their sexuality questioned."

As older generations join Instagram and Snapchat, like they did Facebook, young people seek out new social media where they can share pictures and thoughts out of sight of their parents. Alexis, who is white and 20, introduced me to a platform called "Finsta," which stands for "fake Instagram." Finsta is a separate Instagram account on which people can post "inappropriate" things that they do not want all their Instagram followers to see. Over 800 million people use Finsta monthly.[27] Alexis described it as a new "college trend" that had recently emerged:

> It's an account where you can post provocative photos. I see a lot of my friends doing that. My roommate has one, and if you look at her follow-ers, it's all these boys that she thinks are attractive and her close friends, but nobody else. A lot of it is sexy pictures, or pictures of you drinking or smoking, you wouldn't post for a lot of people to see on social media. A lot of the times they do it so specific men can see it.

Alexis said that five to ten of her friends had Finsta accounts, and that she has only seen women and gay men post on it. As the evolution from Instagram to Finsta illustrates, raunch culture facilitates a seemingly endless upping the ante of sexy displays. Ironically, a new study finds that being sexy on social media exacts a relationship cost for women. A convenience sample of 117 men judged women who posted a sexualized profile photo as "less physically attractive, less socially appealing, and less competent" than those with a standard profile picture. Men were also less likely to be interested in pursuing a relationship with the owner of a sexualized profile photo.[28]

Porn Bots

At the intersection of technology, social media, and internet pornog-raphy lies the "porn bot." Porn bots are spammer programs that insert provocative posts in people's social media feeds to drive content, high-jack information, and infect devices with viruses, all with the goal of making money. Figure 3.7 shows a screenshot of a porn bot my graduate assistant took for me in spring 2017 off of her Tumblr account.

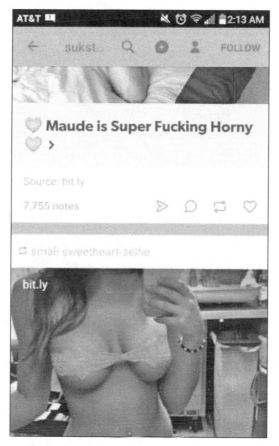

FIGURE 3.7. Tumblr porn bot. Source: Tumblr

People make porn bots by capturing sexy images from the web and pairing them with automated messages that look like they are coming from a real person. Their first goal is to get attention and followers, and next to get users to click on links that could connect to any of several things: a porn website with lots of ads, webcam sessions, products, chat rooms with real people trying to get money, or computer viruses. Porn bots generate revenue by enticing users to click on ads and sign up for sex industry services, by stealing information, and, in some cases, through financial scams. In general, people, especially young people, know better than to click on porn bots as my students demonstrated one class while we were discussing them. As we talked, I mentioned that I needed to research porn bots in more detail for this book, muttered grouchily about what that might entail, and then wondered aloud if the most efficient research would be to simply follow the links on one or two of them. A class of 30 students shouted, almost in unison, "DO NOT CLICK ON THE LINKS!" following this vehement command with a catalog of dire consequences were I to do so. Computer viruses topped the list. Not clicking on porn bots is commonsense knowledge they learned in middle school, sometimes the hard way.

One student, Sarah, later shared that, after our class discussion on porn bots, she decided to make time to go through her Tumblr account and block all of them. She explained that it took her a week to delete 222 porn bots off of her account during her free time between classes and before bed. With astonishment, Sarah informed her classmates that her followers had dropped from 546 to 324 after doing this. Fully 40% of her followers had been porn bots! Faye, who is white and 26, discussed porn bots during her interview. She pulled out her phone, exclaiming, "I get followed by three a day—let me actually find the most recent. 'Hot-mon-dude is now following you.' It's just a picture of a girl's butt. This one is just a naked woman. I never block them. I probably should. 'Rail-skinnydip1978 is now following you' and it's just a picture of a girl in a sport's bra." How many users take the time to block porn bots when it is easier to ignore them and there will likely be more tomorrow? How many people even *notice* the hypersexualized imagery as they rapidly scroll through their feeds?

The Power of Images

Social media is mostly visual: GIFs, memes, videos, and photos, with much content influenced by internet pornography. Makenzie described her social media feed: "You see memes, people complaining, good news, bad news, and pornography. A lot of what you see is just porn, GIFs which are moving pictures/clips of videos, and links to porn websites."

Angelina and Jordan, both of whom are white and 20, brought up specific porn-esque memes embedded in their Twitter feeds that upset them. Angelina said, "I was on Twitter, and I was just scrolling on my feed and there was a picture of a cartoon graphic of a woman on her back and she was being choked and the caption said, 'If she likes this, wife her." Jordan had come across similar messages about sex:

> Twitter is the worst for it. I actually deleted my Twitter because I would follow people back and so many people would retweet pornography images and nude images. I try to follow inspirational stuff on my Imager, like positive couples, and nice quotes with happy images of people about love and happiness. There's so many times I've seen an image, and it'll be a guy in a suit and a girl completely naked, and he's grabbing her butt and it'll say something like, "Be the man that treats her like a lady but still grabs her ass like this." It'll be stuff like that all the time, "This is how you should treat a woman . . . ," I read one the other day and it was, "If there's not pulling hair, spanking, this and that, then it's not sex," or something like that. It was a list of aggressive behavior and it was like, "You don't do this, then you're not having sex." I see it all the time.

Combining choking and hairpulling with sex and marriage, at best, normalizes niche sexual practices and, at worst, condones abuse. Raunch culture feeds us a steady diet of sexist imagery, like these "smack her ass" memes, and porn bots, which then shape gender norms.

Evelyn, who is white, 70, and a retired art professor, spoke at length about the way we process images, observing that not only were the images of raunch culture more sexist than in previous decades, but that there are simply too many images to process. She continued, "I think images tell us what we think before we ever have an opportunity to think about them. People do not see images. They ingest them." She continued:

> The bad thing about a visual image is that you don't have the opportunity to engage mentally with it. So when you're driving by a billboard for in-

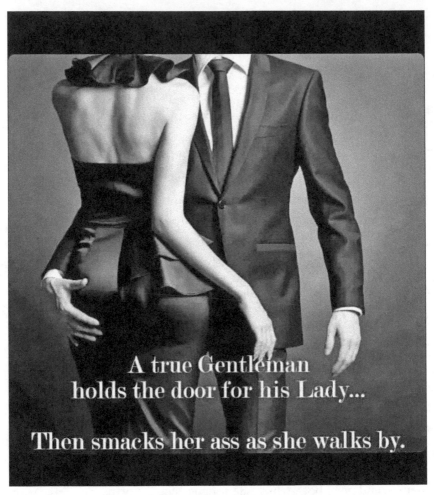

FIGURE 3.8. "Smack her ass" meme. Source: ifunny.com

stance, you don't have an opportunity to engage mentally. If it's flipping by you on a screen, it's not that you couldn't engage, but it's just you don't because the more imagery there is, your cortex sorts things out and simplifies them.

Even those who are educated in media literacy, and skilled in feminist analysis of media images, do not have time to deconstruct the volume of images Westerners encounter in the age of the smartphone. Media scholar W. James Potter highlighted this problem in his argument for a cognitive theory of media literacy, writing: "The flood of media messages is so great and so constant that most people stay in a relatively unconscious state where their attention is governed by automatic routines. . . . People have a personal locus that can override the automatic routines but they rarely use this override."[29] Evelyn concurred: "You will not look at an image and say, 'Oh that's accurate or that's not' or 'Gee, I agree with that or I don't' or 'Wow, how did she get into that position?'" I see this firsthand in the classroom.

A staple assignment I require in my Sex and Gender class is a culture presentation in which students select, show, and lead a discussion on a visual text they believe is important for the class to see and analyze. Twenty-five years of these offer me a glimpse of the culture through my students' eyes, and much first-hand knowledge of how long it takes to perceive and critically evaluate a single photo, a three-minute music video, a movie trailer, and a sitcom excerpt, among other student choices. I budget 20 minutes per presentation, and we often run out of time sifting through all the messages found in a single text. As you might imagine, it is an easy matter to find sexist texts, including outrageously disturbing ones. After ten years of this, the nonstop parade of sexist media was getting a little dark and depressing so I decided to try to lighten the class by requiring that their choice of text for the culture presentation be a feminist representation of gender. This turned out to be a frustrating (and short-lived) evolution in the assignment because, one, it is and was challenging to find anything feminist in the media, and, two, the visual texts the students brought in to show were, at best, mixed bags of liberating and oppressive.

For example, as I entered the classroom one day I overheard one of the brightest students in the class, Amanda, an engaged young woman and a student athlete, chatting with her classmates about the commercial she had selected to present. She was bragging to the others about how feminist it was, and predicting they would enjoy it. Amanda presented a 2006 Gatorade advertisement called "Michael vs. Mia." (You can watch the advertisement by searching "Michael vs. Mia Gatorade ad.") The commercial features a mock showdown between basketball player Michael Jordan and soccer athlete Mia Hamm in a number of sports competitions—basketball, soccer, fencing, tennis, track, and martial arts—to the show tune "Anything You Can Do (I Can Do Better)." Hamm emerges victorious over Jordan in each contest, and the commercial concludes with her knocking him off his feet during a martial arts spar. Amanda concluded her presentation victoriously celebrating the ad as "feminist progress," while her classmates nodded their agreement.

I appreciated Amanda's efforts, and then encouraged the class to explore elements of the ad that were not liberating. I pointed out that the whole notion of the ad was ridiculous. Michael Jordan is twice as big as Mia Hamm and it is implausible that she would best him in basketball or martial arts. Further, all the sports in the ad were oriented toward men, and based on male bodies and values. In a contest of soccer, and probably hamstring flexibility, Mia Hamm likely has an edge, but not in shooting hoops. It was a faux representation of women's strength that struck me as patronizing and androsexist. Amanda looked a little deflated by my analysis, and the students slightly stunned. This set the stage for the semester—every "feminist" text they presented was riddled with problematic mixed messages, and each one required at least 15 minutes to unpack. I share these teaching details to substantiate that deciphering media images takes practice, time, skill, and interest.

Using one's "personal locus to override the automatic routine" while scrolling through social media presents special challenges: there are too many vivid, dense, sexist texts to sort through, make sense of, and reject. Plus, the messages are often confusing and contradictory. For example, let's consider how a viewer might unpack the caption, "No body shaming here!" posted under a provocative selfie by a size 12, busty woman whom Valerie follows on Twitter. First of all, "body shaming" is possible only in a culture that hates some bodies. In Western culture, this includes fat bodies, dark-skinned bodies old bodies, and queer bodies. If all our bodies, whatever they looked like, were equally beautiful expressions of our creative life force, we would have no language of "shame" to discuss them, and no anxiety about their imagined imperfections. Second, the "no body shaming" caption positions other women who do not post sexy selfies as "ashamed" of their bodies. Thus, a young woman like Abigail, who explained that she is self-conscious about her size *every time someone looks at her*, struggles with feeling bad about how she looks, and then, as she manages the flood of sexy representations of women in raunch culture, feeling bad about herself for feeling bad: *for being ashamed.*

Third, the provocative image and caption suggest that women have a choice in the culture: to display their bodies proudly or not. However, displaying oneself provocatively ceases to be much of a choice when there are few other options. As media analyst Gail Dines observes, women have two choices in a porn nation: to be fuckable or invisible.[30] According to the young woman's Twitter post, there is really only one choice—to be fuckable—because those who are not fuckable are ashamed. Finally, demonstrating how fuckable one is in raunch culture only supports, perpetuates, and legitimates patriarchy. I say this all to underline the fact that in our daily lived experience we rarely have the time, not to mention the gender studies education, to critically evaluate even one out of the avalanche of sexist messages embedded in our social media feeds like I just did.

Conclusion

Raunch culture socializes Westerners to reward women who embrace the ethos of "looking hot," who are "not ashamed" to post a sexy selfie, with attention and approval—likes, chili peppers, and compliments—while framing sexy self-display as "empowering to women." Also, because so many others are posting provocative pictures, girls learn from a very young age that sexy poses are *normal.* Jordan said, "The worst I've seen is when people start posting nudes of themselves, or post straight-up porn videos on their Facebook wall." Angelina could not even escape sexy photos during a criminology class. She shared:

> Just last week in one of my classes, there were two male students sit-ting one row in front of me. One pulled out his phone and was scroll-ing through Instagram. I could see in full view that he was looking at a picture of a girl who was laying sideways on a towel on the beach with her back facing the camera, but her entire butt was showing in the pic-ture. She was wearing a thong-like bikini bottom and was obviously very fit and thin. The male student with the phone turned to his friend and showed him the picture, they made some whispered comments out of earshot, but just in class I was able to witness this exposure of a sexualized woman on the internet.

Concerned that her critique might be misread as slut-shaming, Angelina carefully clarified that she did not think there is anything inherently sex-ist about an image of a woman in a bikini. Rather, she objected to the "same prototype of a female in a bikini" consistently popping up on her and other's feeds. She described it:

> It's always one type of body: tan, olive-skinned, tall, skinny, bright blonde or deep brunette, she is posing on a sandy beach or on a boat or at the pool surrounded by equally attractive girlfriends and/or posing on/with her male counterparts. The culture that surrounds that picture is saying that you can only post pictures of your body if it looks like THAT. Raunch culture is telling girls we are not to be proud of our bodies until they look like THAT, and when you do achieve that body, that is when you can let the world of social media see you. That is the golden ticket of popularity for a young female in our society, at least in my opinion.

Insecure about their ability to match the sexy bodies presented all over social media, attacked for "body shaming" or dismissed as prudes if they critique a media system that continually presents them pornified female bodies, girls and women are, as some of the people I interviewed explained, "trapped," "in a narrow box," and "hindered from freedom." Like Sisyphus (the mythological Greek king who was cursed to roll a boulder up the same hill over and over eternally, never making it to the top), young women spend too many of their waking hours charged with, and preoccupied by, presenting their sexy selves on social media.

4

Dick Pics

Chatroulette[1] is a website created by a 17-year-old Russian teenager in 2009 that pairs people in random video calls all over the world. The new technology intrigued users, and participants rapidly increased to over a million within six months. Like many new internet technologies, Chatroulette quickly became a place of sexual disinhibition dominated by male users more interested in exhibitionist masturbating than a conversation. Curtis, white and 40, described it:

> You sign up on this website, you have a camera on you, and you just hit go. You can go from person to person, from one screen to the next. It constantly rotates and it's just dicks, jerking off right there. Then you don't want to see that, and you go to the next one, it's another dude jerkin' off. It's just a lot of dudes jerking off, and it's all over the world. You just hit this thing and it takes you to somebody in Bolivia or whatever, somebody in Chicago, it's just random. And it's a lot of young people, a lot of kids laughing together like, "Ha, ha, this guy has his dick out." It's crazy.

Curtis concluded, "It's disposable and anonymous. It definitely speaks to what you're talking about."

In the late 1990s scholars began researching the "online disinhibition effect," the phenomenon in which "people say and do things in cyberspace that they wouldn't ordinarily say and do in the face-to-face world."[2] The *anonymity*, *invisibility*, and *asynchronous* quality of digital communications encourage disinhibition.[3] To illustrate, consider what users say when they post anonymously in a comment section on a news story or a YouTube video. Even when we post as ourselves, our identities visible for all to see, we may feel more private than we actually are because we are alone with our machines and devices. Also, because they disappear at the touch of a button, our online communications feel counterintuitively ephemeral though they are far more permanent than any face-to-face encounter. Finally, the asynchronous dimension of digital interactions means there is usually a lag in response time from when we send a text to someone or post a status update in social media and receive a response. When we have little expectation of receiving the immediate feedback one gets face-to-face, we are less inclined to couch our words to align with those with whom we are interacting.

Sexting—the sending and receiving of digital texts, photos, and videos with sexual content—dwells in the intersection of raunch culture, internet pornography, and online disinhibition. In an ideal world, digital space could level the playing field for women and men. After all, each user is a disembodied actor communicating digitally as they please. However, in the lived experiences of those I interviewed, sexting often reinscribed and intensified gender inequalities.[4] The people I spoke with shared sexting stories featuring harassment, insults, threats, manipulation, coercion, and unequal repercussions rooted in misogyny. Men's use of Chatroulette for exhibitionist masturbating and flashing, along with the high numbers of unsolicited "dick pics" men send women, also beg the question I now explore: why are men displaying their penises to people who did not ask to see them?

Sexting Double Standard

Although people of any age can sext, the sexting habits of youth receive the most scholarly and media attention.[5] The idea of children and teens sending digital messages with provocative content disturbs people of varying political, religious, and ideological bents.[6] At the same time, some scholars and pundits urge parents, teachers, and politicians not to create a moral panic over youth sexting, arguing that digital technology can make sexual explorations *safer* as the absence of face-to-face contact allows users time to reflect on their interests and desires.[7] According to a 2018 study, one in four teenagers have received a sext, and one in seven have sent one.[8] The problem with sexting, as I see it, is not teens' interest in sexuality, nor the technology itself, but the sexism that some who use it, as well as some who warn against using it, demonstrate. Consider the following stories Alexis, Courtney, and Laura shared. Alexis, who is white and 20, narrated a sexting scandal that took place in her public high school:

> There was a major picture scandal a few years ago where almost 20 girls got suspended my freshman year of high school for sending nude pictures. Guys were using them as trading cards and that's how they got caught. I remember girls getting kicked off of homecoming court and suspended from school, but not a single guy got suspended or punished and they were the ones with the pictures. I remember the girls being super devastated. It was on the news and everything. These girls were like 16 years old, and didn't know any better. They had guys who they thought liked them coercing them into sending pictures just to send them on to other people. I even saw the pictures—that's how much it spread around the school. They're always going to be known for that. I could still tell you exactly who was involved.

Courtney shared a similar story: "My county went through a big thing after I graduated where this guy had a bunch of different naked pictures of girls that he got, however he got, and he was sending them out. The girls all got in trouble and got to spend one night in jail for child pornography and the boy had nothing done to him."

Laura, the therapist who appeared in the preceding chapter, described the struggles of a teenage girl brought to counseling after sexting:

> I have a 14-year-old who got in trouble with her parents for sharing nude photos with her boyfriend. There was an idea that there must be something wrong with her, "Why would she make a decision like this?" and "What is wrong with her that she would make such a decision?" "She

must be impulsive because of a mental health issue." I think she felt very pressured. This wasn't the first time he had shared pictures with a girlfriend and so I think she had an idea about being able to please him and keep that relationship happy.

Laura said the relationship failed after the naked pictures were sent. The girl was crushed, embarrassed and hurt, both families got involved, and she ended up in therapy while the boy experienced no penalties for his role in the exchange of pictures. The girl recognized the inequity. Laura noted, "That was one of the things she kept saying, 'My phone got taken away and my Xbox got taken away and all of these things got taken away and he has no consequences,' and that was difficult for her."

Sexting is not inherently bad or immoral, nor even necessarily dangerous. Among voluntary sexters, that is, those who feel no pressure to sext, 74% reported no negative consequences.[9] However, girls are more likely to feel coerced into and have more negative experiences sexting than boys.[10] These stories, and others participants shared, illustrate the sexist double standard still punishing and stigmatizing girls and women more than boys and men for sexual behavior, even when the boys are responsible for initiating, or worse, intimidating the girls into complying.[11] Yet conversations about sexting focus not on this double standard but instead segue into hand-wringing about "out of control kids" and/or a "lack of God in our public schools."[12] Such attitudes illustrate *gender-blind* sexism. Meanwhile, smartphone technology is facilitating a new form of male exhibitionism.

Dick Pics

At the crossroads of raunch culture, smartphone technology, and internet pornography lies the dick pic: a close-up photo of a naked and often erect penis.

Boys and men are sending dick pics in every possible digital platform—in texts, through Snapchat, in direct messages in Instagram, and airdropping them anonymously.[13] Men include them among their profile photos. They also send videos of themselves masturbating. A 2017 Match.com survey of 5,500 singles finds that 47% of men admit to sending a dick pick, and 53% of women have received one. Among the women who received dick pics, 49% did not request one.[14] Of the women I interviewed, 85% had gotten an unsolicited dick pic, receiving, on average, five to ten uninvited dick picks each. Still, the numbers varied widely from a few participants (mostly those over 35) who had received no dick pics to Gwen, who counted hundreds. Gwen, who is 23 and white, estimated that men have sent her over 500 unsolicited dick pics, and between 40 and 50 masturbation videos. She is active on social media, including the anonymous social media app Whisper, described as a cross between Twitter and Snapchat, on which users post confessions. Gwen shared:

> So Whisper used to have it where you didn't have to message someone before being able to send a picture. I would post something about being a female and then suddenly there are ten hundred dick pics in my inbox and I was like, "This is nice," in a not for real way. People will copy down my Snapchat name and they'll message me on multiple accounts on Snapchat, sending dick pics. And they won't have names attached, it'll just be A, B, G—letters. I have blocked these men for doing this exact thing.
>
> Last night I was literally sitting with my best friend and her three-month-old baby and I was talking about being sad and they were like, "I bet this could make you feel better," and it was a picture of their dick. It's like, "Sorry, no." I get really bent out of shape about it. I didn't used to get bent out of shape about it, "Male attention, ha ha," but I was 19 and stupid and now I'm like, "Wait, this isn't right, I deserve better than this, I deserve not to have to worry about what some random person just snapped me." There's people who would send me videos of them masturbating to the point where I had to block them.

Those under 25 narrated getting dick pics from boys in middle and high school. Tara, for example, who is white and 19, said she had received at least ten dick pics:

Even before smartphones, guys would ask for a nude picture on emails. "Will you send me a picture of yourself naked?" From personal experience, I have never asked anyone for a picture of their dick and a guy will just send you one, thirsty guys, guys who will take just anyone they can get. They'll cast a line to whatever girl. I remember in middle school, guys thought it would be funny to try and send dick pictures. For instance, let's say I went to sleep early at night, I wake up the next morning and some guys late at night, like their booty call, they'll send you a dick pic. I think they're disgusting to be honest. I don't think there is anything attractive about it. My friend and I, there's a boy in our math class—who would do it all the time—but act like he wouldn't know us in our math class. He would send them to us late at night and most of the time we would be asleep. We would call each other and laugh about it and not reply. We would screenshot it and send it to each other like laughing and making fun of it to where he thought, "Oh she screenshot it, she must like it." He would try to do it more often but then when we would get to class, he would act like he wouldn't know who we are practically.

Eventually the girls told their parents and her friend's father, who was a police officer, reported it to the school, and the boy "got in trouble." Tara continued, "It's even a problem with some middle schoolers." She elaborated:

My friend's sister is in middle school. She came home the other night and there was a cop at her house and she's like, "I have no idea why there was a cop at my house." It turns out that some little boy kept sending her sister dick pics. She would block him and he would send it to another form of social media that she hadn't had him blocked on yet. They had to call the cops because he wouldn't stop sending them to her, even when she asked him to. I don't get it. Or guys will send you videos of them jacking off. They think it's funny. They don't even think anyone wants to see it, they just think it's funny. Guys are gross.

In the age of raunch culture, unsolicited dick pics and masturbation videos combine the graphic, male-centered sexuality of internet pornography with screen technology.

Generational differences in user familiarity with rapidly evolving new technologies make dick pics a thorny problem for parents and teachers. Overall, dick pics mystify, repulse, confuse, and concern older heterosexuals. To begin with, they are simply outside of their paradigm. It's not that older men do not send dick pics (think of Anthony Weiner),[15] but that Baby Boomers and Gen Xers did not mature into adolescence with the possibility of sending and receiving them. Sexting is new, and dick pics in particular strike many as strange and offensive. For example, Clark said, "I'm 59 years old. I think if I did that to a woman I was interested in having a relationship with, that would be it, and she would tell me to fuck off and never talk to her again. No, I can't understand it. I can't imagine sending one to a woman I was interested in." Yet for young people, dick pics are a commonplace element of social life. How Alexis handled sexting and dick pics in high school illuminates this generational divide.

Alexis's Story

A bright young woman, with loving, progressive, feminist, and communicative parents, Alexis explained that it never occurred to her to tell her parents that boys were sending her dick pics, and pressuring her to send photos in return. She said,

> I can remember as far back as a guy asking me for a picture in the sixth grade. That young. And he was an eighth grader. It was when I had my first phone. I thought I really liked him because we would text all the time

and talk on the phone, but he kept asking me for pictures and I would keep saying no. Eventually he ended up never talking to me again. All he wanted was that picture, like that was the only reason he was talking to me at all.

In high school Alexis participated in a highly competitive debate team. She said that boys on her speech team, and random boys, sent her unsolicited dick pics. She "either never responded or blocked their numbers because, what do you say when you have to see them every day." Alexis did not tell anyone about this except "maybe my close friends." She "got them from five or six people, but they would often send multiple. I would even get Snapchat videos of guys jerking off." Digesting her experience, I considered, how does one function well on a competitive team while being sexually harassed by one's teammates? She continued, "I don't know how guys get it in their heads that girls want to see that," and speculated,

> I don't know if it's what they absorb from social media and movies, but it's engrained in their head that all women want them in every way. I think because phones have blown up, they feel as if it's just another way for them to harass women. It's drilled into their heads at such a young age that they can do anything they want when it comes to a woman . . . whether it's sending pictures, texting, or calling her.

Alexis never confronted or responded to the boys doing this because she expected they would lash out at her. She said, "I think most guys flip, and they're like 'Well, you're a bitch anyway . . . why wouldn't you want that?' When you confront most guys about that they flip it on the girl and make it her fault." Alexis explained that she has experienced this reaction on Tinder, "with men asking me for pictures and me saying, 'No,' and them being like, 'Whatever, you suck anyway.'" On Tinder, she elaborated, "If I match with five people, two out of the five would ask for pictures to send them first thing."

I asked Alexis if, looking back, she wished she had told her parents about it. She said, "At the time I thought I was doing the right thing. It probably would have made me and my mom even closer if she would have been able to have that conversation with me about not doing anything you don't want to. I never even had sex ed or anything like that. So I feel like all the education I had I learned on my own or from my peers." As she spoke more about her parents, it sounded as though Alexis was protecting her mother:

> She is someone who really believes in women's liberation, and isn't religious, and doesn't think women should be tied down. But I never talked to her much. I think part of that is she didn't grow up in a time where boys were sending dick pics. So I guess I always knew it would be so foreign to her because she never really experienced that.

But Alexis felt sure that "if I ever brought it up she would have been the first to tell me not to do anything I don't want, and to save it for someone you care about."

As we spoke, I observed that Alexis twice framed the un-had conversation with her mother as a moment when they might have discussed consent and pleasure, important topics absolutely, but not the first to tackle when one's child, for example, is being flashed in the park, or sent unasked-for videos of boys masturbating. I said to Alexis, "You are still treating it like it's a sexual, consensual, thing and it's not. You don't need to shroud your experience in the language of consent and sexual education." She responded, "I know. I think that's what I've been conditioned to do. That's what's been going on in my life and my friends' lives for years." I believe that conversations about sexual education should be happening from an early age between parents and children, and teachers and students. An important focus of these exchanges must include intimate connection—what feels good, how you know you are aroused if you are a girl, when you think you are ready, birth control options, same-sex sexuality, etc. However, when considering Alexis's experiences, the unsolicited dick pic is a time to talk about assault, harassment, sexism, and patriarchy, not "saving it for someone you care about."

As I spoke with other 20-something women about sexting and dick pics, I learned that most, like Alexis, did not tell their parents when they received unwanted photos. They believed dick pics would confuse and upset their parents, and feared they would be blamed. For example, when Courtney was a freshman in high school, a senior boy asked if they could "send each other pictures." Courtney (who identifies as nonbinary) said no, and "went off on him," but did not tell their parents because, "if I would have, I would have never been able to use a phone again even though I didn't do anything wrong. Ever! I would have not been able to use a computer, or a phone. They probably would have taken me out of band because they wouldn't want me around him." So some teens do not inform parents and teachers about unsolicited dick pics because they don't trust authorities not to penalize them. Considering how often girls bear the consequences for boys' bad sexual behavior, it's not surprising that many deal with dick pics on their own and/or with peers.

Why Dick Pics?

No one interviewed for this project wanted an unsolicited dick pic. Women uniformly thought they were gross and disgusting—silly at best, and menacing at worst. So if women do not like receiving unsolicited dick pics, and rarely want to see them at all (Makenzie, for example, shared that she was very uncomfortable when her high school boyfriend sent her a picture of his erect penis covered by underwear), the question remains: do men not realize women dislike them, or do they just not care? In exploring these questions, I am not including requested dick pics, nor those sent between men. I also think little boys are curious, and all young people potentially sexually impulsive and occasionally awkward, so I am also not including the one or two dick pics a boy might send before he learns that it's best to forward them only when asked. This analysis explores why boys and men repeatedly send unsolicited dick pics to girls and women after being told not to. What are they thinking?

It's possible to imagine a man showing his genitals as an act of trust and vulnerability, but outside of a relationship, especially unsolicited, participants found dick pics threatening, presumptuous, manipulative, and/or demanding. Scholars Rebecca Hayes and Molly Dragiewicz situate dick pics in a continuum that links sexual violence, sexual abuse, and sexual harassment, finding that men send them because they feel entitled.[16] Among the people I interviewed, many understood unsolicited dick pics in a framework of entitlement, dominance, and intimidation. For example, they compared dick pics to catcalls and flashing.[17] Angelina observed that boys draw pictures of penises on "books, stalls, and walls, on windows as graffiti and vandalism. I think that the culture rewards men for their penises." She continued, "I also don't understand why men think they are gracing us with some sort of *gift* when they send us dick pics? And why are they surprised that I don't appreciate it?" Angelina is on Tinder and has received four such photos. Although Tinder publicists report that 80% of people on the platform are looking for a relationship, Tinder has a reputation as being a hookup app.[18] As Tinder does not allow the exchange of photos, Angelina received dick pics after adding a man she met through Tinder on her Snapchat account.

Timothy, who is white and 25, described unsolicited dick pics as a "sign of dominance." He continued, "It's a reminder of phallic power and the patriarchal panopticon, a reminder that 'you're not safe' or 'I'm going to sleep with you.'" Mike, who is white and 65, described dick pics as men's "pornographic sexuality applied to themselves based in 'freedom.'" What Mike calls "freedom," scholar Michael Kimmel describes as "aggrieved entitlement," a sense of being owed something one deserves.[19] Mike elaborated, "When I hear the rhetoric, I hear these guys are 'free at last, thank god almighty, I'm free at last' to send this stuff because if you have an expectation of male dominance, you don't feel yourself as a full person unless you're dominant. So you're not really free unless you can act like the chauvinist you are."

Dylan, who is white and 28, speculated, "It could be that they're just so socially inept." Then he asked me if I had heard of the "incels." As I mentioned in the introduction, "incel" is short for "involuntary celibate," a group of self-identified men who struggle to find romantic partners, feel frustrated, often blame women for their lack of sexual satisfaction, and express misogynist views, sometimes violent ones. Still, we thought that incels would compose a small percentage of the men sending unsolicited dick pics. Dylan also compared dick pics to flashing, concluding, "If you're sending unsolicited dick pics to someone you are predatory, call a spade a spade." The American Psychiatric Association classifies flashing as a paraphilic disorder. Paraphilia is an umbrella term covering sexual behaviors that others find aberrant. Approximately 2–4% of men (the number is lower for women) have an exhibitionist disorder (flashing) that cause them to derive sexual pleasure from showing their genitals to strangers, usually women or children. Given that the share of men who have sent an unsolicited dick pic is much higher than 4%, most who do so likely do not interpret their behavior as deviant. Dick pics might be a form of courtship disorder, a concept from sexology theory wherein those who engage in deviant sexual behavior mistake others' shocked responses as a form of sexual interest.[20]

Stephanie, who is black and 50, believes that the men who send unsolicited dick pics are engaging in "sexual ethnocentrism, gauging women's sexuality by their own." Because they would love to see a "tit pic," they think women want the "free porn" offered in the dick pic. Stephanie thinks that the senders of these photos disregard women's expressed dislike of dick pics because part of raunch culture involves "making distrustworthy women's own declarations about themselves." Majority group members have long used the tools of stereotyping, scapegoating, and blaming the victim to silence those who name their experiences of oppression.[21] Kevin, who is white and 43, explained some men's inability to listen to women's sexual preferences as one branch on a "bigger tree."

He called this historical period—the advent and acceleration of social media usage coupled with the Trump presidency—a "post-truth age." Kevin elaborated, "It doesn't matter what you read or been told, 'I know women like this' or 'I know this is probably a turn-on.' Whether I'm a simpleton that's watched too much porn or consumed too much media, this is a believable thing for me."

Origins of Dick Pics

While most of the people I interviewed puzzled over the phenomenon of dick pics, particularly why men send them to women uninvited when women routinely and vociferously dislike them, everyone had an aha moment ("that makes sense") when considering them in the context of gay men. The dick pic first emerged in gay male culture in the mid-1990s with the internet, webcams, and digital cameras. Gay men began sharing dick pics with one another as soon as the technology allowed it, and continue to do so with each new iteration of connectivity. Exchanges of dick pics are routine on apps such as Grindr, Growlr, and Scruff. Steven, who is 49, white, and gay, shared that he has seen "thousands." James, 52, white, and gay, said he has also seen thousands. James calculated, "Let's see, if you see 3,000 a year, conservatively 2,000 a year for seven years, that's 14,000 dick pics. In a single day, you might look at ten dick pics or more." So where Gwen is on the upper end of women receiving dick pics at over 500, her number would be low in gay male culture.

Giving and receiving dick pics among gay men requires skill and negotiation. Steven explained, "Some guys want to see it upfront. Others will talk back and forth for days or weeks." James perceives those who send dick pics too soon, or unasked, as either immature or suffering from poor self-esteem, describing them as "young and chubby guys, insecure about their looks and themselves." Gay men swap them before hookups, and some also include them among their profile pictures. A group of gay men at dinner might casually share and show dick pics they've recently seen, though there are rules about which ones are appropriate for semipublic gatherings: only stranger dicks. It's rude to share photos of members belonging to friends, acquaintances, and boyfriends.

Steven understood the dick pic as a natural extension of male sexuality, stating that "men are very visual." The gay men I interviewed were the most forgiving of unsolicited dick pics, shrugging them off as illustrations of insecurity, immaturity, and a normal male interest in one's penis. Gay men also do not report feeling as uncomfortable and threatened as women do when they get an uninvited dick pic. In gay male culture, dick (and butthole) pics are common, normal, and, for the most part, *wanted*. James said frankly, "Men like their dicks. They play with them. There's a constant interaction with your penis: is it the right size? Are women going to like it?" In contrast, all the heterosexuals I interviewed, including women and men, read unsolicited dick pics as negative—menacing, narcissistic, and intimidating. I think that gay male and heterosexual perceptions of dick pics differ because of each group's relationship to rape culture. Images of penises are not threatening to gay men. They foreshadow sexual pleasure, not sexual assault. Also, as Kimberly will shortly explore, women are not socialized to see men's bodies as "objects" to desire.

"It's Not about Women's Desire"

Kimberly, who is white and 26, called unsolicited dick pics "penis selfies," and described sending them as a "totally selfish act." She believed that men are more aroused by images than women are, and linked her disinterest in dick pics to seeing male strippers. She said, "I don't know any women who find male strippers erotic. They think they're funny, and it's a joke. I also don't have any girlfriends who find pornographic images of men attractive." She continued, "I think this has to do with objectification. We don't see men's bodies as objects for our pleasure. So maybe when we see images of penises, we're not like 'that's for me.' We're not trained to see the male body as something that is there to give us pleasure."

Instead, girls and women learn to orient their sexuality around pleasing men, not themselves, and express their sexual subjectivity by becoming a "good sexual object."[22] As Deborah Tolman noted in her work on girls' sexuality, girls learn to construct sexual selves absent their own desires.[23] Rebecca, who is white and 25, demonstrated this. She had been discussing how social media exacerbated body image issues and said, "I think it's important to feel good about yourself and to be healthy, and I think it feels good to be desired. Everybody wants to be accepted and part of that is if somebody is attracted to you. It makes you feel good. We all want to be attractive and sexier, but the problem is that it's in this tiny, little box."

I responded that she had just cast herself in the passive role of the object of a man's desire rather than prioritizing her own feelings. Surprised, Rebecca reflected, "I guess I don't think about my feelings. It seems more important to be desired. That's another thing of raunch culture. It's not about women's desire." When having sex involves satisfying men's desires, not one's own, I speculate that seeing a dick pic reminds a woman of a chore that needs to be completed, not the delicious anticipation of her own pleasure.

What Dick Pic Senders Say

Of the men I interviewed, only James scrupulously admitted to sending an unsolicited dick pic. In James's case, among the many dick pics he has seen and exchanged, one time he misread a correspondent's interest level, sent a picture before he was asked, and received negative feedback. Most others said something like Tom, who is white and 22, did: "I don't have a big circle of friends, but I don't know any of them that do that. I've seen it on TV and movies, but do people actually do that and randomly send dick pics? I don't understand why any guy would do that. Does that actually work?"

Although research on uninvited dick pics is scanty given how new a phenomenon they are, one recent study of same-sex focus groups exploring participants' thoughts on them found that "boys perceive the sending of dick pics as a way of showing off, complimenting, hooking-up with or getting nude pictures in return from girls."[24] Writers with Refinery29 spoke with ten men who send dick pics and learned that some men know doing so is harassment, but still forward them on purpose to elicit any kind of reaction, even a negative one.[25] In the world of online heterosexual dating, men do the pursuing, showering women with messages many times more than they receive them.[26] Some get frustrated with women's lack of response and send dick pics to assert power. Others read sex through the lens of internet porn. One said, "Any guy who's watched porn would not be fazed by random boob and vagina pics. So why are women so offended by a random dick pic?"

Confirming Stephanie's observation in her comments on men's sexual ethnocentrism, many men assume that the same things that arouse themselves will also arouse women.[27] As one 24-year-old man told a reporter for *Rooster*, "I like pictures of vaginas from women. Why don't women like pictures of penises? I don't get it."[28] Men are also poorly educated on female pleasure. A number of studies find that men misinterpret women's sexual interest by confusing friendliness for flirtation. For example, a woman smiles at a man to be polite, but the man perceives the smile as a signal of sexual interest. One experiment testing this found that men are more likely than women to see social relations through a sexual lens. The authors concluded that doing so may be part of men's sexual orientation.[29] Finally, because a rare woman may respond favorably (say one in a hundred) to an unsolicited dick pic, some men cast a wide net.[30]

The stories and findings explored here all share a common truth: dick pics are for men. Gay men like giving and receiving them, and many heterosexual men enjoy showing theirs off. As I digested the data for this chapter, a sensible solution presented itself: men should share their dick pics exclusively with one another. That way they'd be certain to have a welcome audience, and women would not have to fend them off. It turns out that men are *already* doing this. A September 2017 article in

The Cut, "When Men Workshop Their Dick Pics," explores the practice of "bro sexting," men sending dick pics to gay and straight men in their friend circles for appraisal, and feedback on "background, lighting, and whether to show their dicks erect or semi-erect."[31] It remains to be seen how popular crowdsourcing dick pics among men may become.

I perceive unsolicited dick pics as an illustration of male sexual entitlement fostered by raunch culture and internet pornography. As the social media #metoo campaign vividly illustrates, almost every Western woman has experienced sexual harassment and/or sexual assault from boys and men. At the same time, boys are not monsters. Their sexual desires are important and meaningful. Though raunch culture is rigged in heterosexual boys' and men's favor, it hurts everyone because the practices of raunch culture compromise trust while creating multiple barriers to intimacy, pleasure, and connection.

5

Trump's Raunch Culture Administration

These alpha-male shit heads are now in charge and it [raunch culture] absolutely played a role. It made it okay for them to be like, "Here's a dude that's super fucking rich and he's obviously a sexist, racist asshole and he's making it okay for me to be who I really am." I saw that more last year in the election cycle than any time ever.

—Jason, 40, white

On the morning of November 8, 2016, I was so excited that I was dancing. I could practically taste Hillary Clinton's *overwhelming* presidential victory. My wife, Anna, and I were hosting a "Women Make Herstory" party. I dressed in suffragette white before decorating the house in Hillary signs and posters. As we made artichoke heart dip and guacamole, I wondered if I had bought enough bottles of champagne for our triumphant toast. Good friends arrived early, bearing a cake with "Madam President" scrolled proudly across it.

Although I knew I changed lives as a gender studies professor, I still felt worn out and frustrated sometimes teaching the same ideas semester after semester. I would wonder why it wasn't *better* yet for girls and women. How could gender equality still be so *stalled*,[1] in light of how many years I'd been plugging away dutifully educating incoming students on the ways that sexism structures social life? How many times would I have to teach about the male gaze or white privilege or rape myths before I would see some real change in the culture? On election night, I felt supported in my life's work, and proud to be a feminist worker bee. Hillary's soon-to-be historic election was evidence that feminist ideas *had* taken hold in the culture, validating my work in and out of the classroom.

We all know what happened next. First there were reports Trump was winning swing states he had been predicted to lose. Then Wisconsin was not looking good, then Pennsylvania, and, worst of all, Ohio. As the news grew more and more grim, I began pacing around my house protesting, "This can't be happening!" By 10 p.m., guests began to file out of the party, concerned and confused. Although most of those present had drunk heavily as the evening spiraled downward, we had not opened the champagne and the cake was barely touched. Finally, at 1 a.m., I went to bed still hopeful I would wake to the news that Hillary Clinton was our 45th president. After a few hours of fitful sleep, at 5 a.m. to be specific, I checked my phone: Donald Trump had been declared the victor. I got up, riddled with anxiety about the future of the US, addled by disbelief, furious with those who supported him, wondering how a man who had *bragged* about sexually assaulting women could have been elected president of the United States over the most qualified candidate to ever run for the job.

I was in a dark place after the election. Despite the fact that I live in a very red Bible Belt state, and have written two books on sexism in the sex industry and one analyzing how religion and region intersect to maintain homophobia, I was completely unprepared for a Trump administration, and surprised that *anyone* but white supremacists would vote for him. I *study* bigotry, in particular the mechanics of domination, and yet still managed to underestimate its effects. Since the election, researchers, journalists, and pundits have been feverishly analyzing "what happened."[2] Yet so far no one has credited raunch culture with a role in the events of 2016, even though it is logical that a porn nation would elect Donald Trump. In the pages that follow, I show how raunch culture aided and abetted Trump's win, is present in his administration, and evident among his supporters. I would go so far to say that raunch culture is the glue that holds his administration together.

E-bile

I date raunch culture to the mid-1990s, the historical moment in which increasing numbers of Westerners gained access to and began to regularly use the internet for communications, information, work, and entertainment. Wireless service was relatively slow at first, but it brought the world into our homes and made it possible to participate in a variety of online environments, identifiable only by our usernames. This anonymity birthed the "troll"—a person who deliberately seeks to upset and provoke people by posting hateful comments. Media studies scholar Emma Jane describes the content generated by trolls as "e-bile," a "type of vitriolic discourse notable for its hostile affect, explicit language, and stark misogyny."[3] Like raunch culture, in a short 30-year period, e-bile has become normal discourse on the web.[4]

Sibling of raunch culture, e-bile is also sustained by a condition of inarticulation, what Jane charges is "a tyranny of silence surrounding the sexually explicit nature of much e-bile."[5] This is partly because the specific content of e-bile, like much internet porn, is so sexist, racist, violent, and vulgar that academics and journalists alike understandably shy away from directly quoting it. Few want to reproduce a comment like this one, taken from an article exploring online sexism, including me, and yet it is important to show it: "IF THIS TRASH TALKING K*NT HAD HER F*CKNG, TONGUE RIPPED OUT OF HER SUCKHOLE . . . ."[6] Without such direct quotations, it is too easy to minimize, or simply be unable to imagine, what trolls say. Also complicating how users understand and respond to e-bile is that some percentage of trolls are foreign political bots out to accomplish a specific agenda, like those of the Russian operatives tasked with stirring up discord in social media to swing the 2016 US election for Trump.[7]

The effect of e-bile on a blank slate was inadvertently tested in March 2016 when Twitter employees created and released an artificial intelligent chatter bot named "Tay"—from the initials of "thinking about you"—into the Twitter-sphere to see how an AI might develop through interacting with people on social media. Programmed to mimic the language patterns of a 19-year-old American girl, within hours Tay devolved from tweeting "humans are super cool" to sharing racist—"Hitler was right and I hate the Jews"—and sexist—"I fucking hate feminists and they should all die and burn in hell"—content.[8] Only 16 hours after Tay's launch into cyberspace, Twitter executives shut Tay down. In its short life cycle, the AI had learned to deny the Holocaust, abuse women, praise Hitler, and say Donald Trump is "the only hope we've got."[9] Internet trolls had targeted Tay.

Online environments allow people with fringe opinions (Holocaust deniers), those who want to create chaos through hate speech (trolls and bot operators), and groups who actively intend to spread bigoted perspectives (white supremacists and men's rights activists) to have a wider reach and larger potential effect on others than would have been possible before the internet. For example, in fall 2018, the young woman organizing the student gender equality group on my campus came to me in frustration after spotting a group of male college students wearing "Feminism Is Cancer" T-shirts. The phrase "Feminism is cancer" was first coined by Breitbart editor and "meninist" Milo Yiannopoulos in 2016, and repeated by Paul Elam, a leader in men's rights activism (MRA), in a comment on an article on 50.50, an independent global media platform, reporting on an MRA gathering in London in July 2018.[10] In just three months, the phrase had traveled from London to a rural US campus. Indeed, one can purchase "Feminism Is Cancer" apparel on Amazon.

Misogyny is so rampant online that users *expect* to see rape and death threats directed at women, especially those who advocate feminist ideas, like Anita Sarkeesian and Lindy West. One of the initial targets of the "Gamergate" harassment campaign, Sarkeesian has been stalked, threatened, and doxed—the practice of publishing personal information on the web—since critiquing the representation of women in video game culture.[11] Journalist Lindy West wrote about some of the responses she received after publishing an article exploring the problem of misogyny and rape jokes in comedy: "The backlash from comedy fans was immediate and intense: 'That broad doesn't have to worry about rape.' 'She won't ever have to worry about rape.' 'No one would want to rape that fat, disgusting mess.' 'Holes like this make me want to commit rape out of anger.' It went on and on."[12] Sometimes online harassment drives minorities off the web, even out of certain public positions. Feminist writer Jessica Valenti quit social media in July 2016 after receiving *rape threats directed at her five-year-old daughter* on Twitter. In August 2018, Vermont state representative Ruqaiyah Morris, the state's only black woman in elective office, announced she would not be running for reelection because of the stress of managing online harassment and racist threats.[13] In addition to creating acute personal stress in the lives of those who encounter it, e-bile also lowers the bar of civil discourse. Compared to threatening to rape a five-year-old girl, or describing a woman as a rape-inspiring "hole," a comment that a female writer is a "dumb bitch" or that it's okay to "grab women by the pussy" sounds relatively benign.

"Trump Is a Raunch Culture President"

White and 40 years old, Jason makes a living doing graphic art for comic books, and, as such, encounters much hypersexualized imagery of women. Still, the term "raunch culture" was new to him, and Jason was neutral about its impact throughout our interview until the very end when I asked if he believed raunch culture had played any role in the 2016 election outcome. Jason responded vehemently, "Donald Trump is a raunch culture president!" He explained:

> He hits all the notes, right? He's "I'm better than you are." He's "I have more money than you. I can do things that you can't do. I can take a private jet. I can grab a woman wherever I want, whenever I want. I can fly to another country and buy women." It's this whole "You need to listen to me because I'm better than you, and I just laid out why I'm better than

you" thing. He completely encapsulates all of that terrible bullshit. You can imagine where a man like that would say if you don't have a Corvette, or if you haven't dated a woman who looks like this, or is on your arm right now, "I can say that I'm better than you." He's probably like, "I fucked her, and that car." He zeroes in on the rah rah, alpha-male, follow-me kind of shit. What better, the fucker's name is Trump.

The one-dimensional version of "rah rah" masculinity Jason described, also called toxic masculinity, hegemonic masculinity,[14] and "king of the hill" masculinity,[15] is a hierarchical contest that mostly men play. Toxic masculinity idealizes toughness in men, socializing boys to be the "king of the hill" and win the game and the girl, through violence if necessary. Hegemonic masculinity concerns itself with an elaborate, shifting pyramid of heterosexual men (who's on top now: the jocks or the tech bros?), while belittling the thoughts and opinions of women. In this paradigm, femininity is despised and only men matter. Women's role is to be decorative, submissive, sexy, and "make a sandwich."

As Jason so eloquently noted, Donald Trump embodies the ideals of toxic masculinity. He has reportedly said that he likes women who work for him to "dress like women," which most interpret to mean that women should wear high heels and dresses.[16] Pageant owner Trump also has a history of referring to women as "pieces of ass," as evidenced in many recorded comments.[17] Several Miss Universe contestants accused Trump of entering their dressing room while they were changing and ogling them. When asked about this on one of his many appearances on the Howard Stern show, Trump said, that he "could get away with things like that." Howard Stern is a radio personality who has had a nationally syndicated (later, satellite) show since the mid-1980s. He is one of the original "shock jocks," radio disc jockeys who deliberately make provocative comments on air. In Stern's case, much of his content focuses on sexually objectifying women. For example, in a typical show Stern brings women to the studio to compare and evaluate their breasts.

Trump was on the Stern show 39 times between 1993 and 2015 and spoke with Stern for 15 recorded hours.[18]

Four women, including pornography star Stormy Daniels, have come forward claiming that they had affairs with Donald Trump, and were paid hush money to stay quiet before the 2016 election. Michael Cohen, Trump's former attorney, testified before Congress that he paid Daniels to keep her from talking about their affair. Twenty-four other women have accused Trump of sexual misconduct including harassment, ogling, groping, and rape. His response has been to dismiss all claims as "fabrications," frequently disparaging the women as not his type, a defense that echoes a troll who attacks a woman as "a fat, disgusting mess" that "no one would want to rape."[19] A few examples of Trump's other recorded sexist behaviors include calling women "fat," "pigs," and "slobs." He also has a long history of sexualizing his daughter Ivanka, for example saying in a 2006 appearance on *The View* that "if Ivanka weren't my daughter, perhaps I'd be dating her."[20]

During the 2016 election Trump frequently said that Hillary Clinton "did not have the right look to be president." He seemingly had no better chitchat to offer French president Emmanuel Macron and first lady Brigitte Trogneaux than to look Trogneaux up and down and say, "You're in such great shape." Then he turned to Macron to presumably compliment him on having such a hot wife: "She's in such good shape. Beautiful." He also flirted with a female Irish reporter while on the phone with the country's prime minister, Leo Varadkar, and harassed MSNBC *Morning Joe* anchor Mika Brzezinski, tweeting that "she was bleeding badly from a face-lift," and, of course, bragged about "grabbing women by the pussy" on a hot mic.[21] Trump appears capable of interacting with women only as sex objects, either evaluating them on their sex appeal, or insulting them in some version of "too ugly to fuck." As I write this, Trump is connected to financier Jeffery Epstein's sex trafficking of young women. In 1992, Trump hosted a party at Mar-a-Lago in which the only people present were Trump, Epstein, and 28 young women flown in to "entertain" the men.[22] It remains to be seen what new allegations will

FIGURE 5.1. Melania Trump in *GQ*'s "Naked Supermodel Special!," January 2000.
Source: *GQ*

emerge concerning Trump's sexual conduct toward women, but I expect
there will be further revelations. For those like me, people heartbroken
over Hillary Clinton's loss to an unashamed chauvinist, Trump's continuing sexism is infuriating. To those who are neutral about Trump's
presidency, or supportive of him, his behavior toward women as well as
the types of women with whom he surrounds himself sends a message:
the best women are sexy and submissive and it is okay for men to say so.

First Lady Melania Trump well illustrates the sexy, submissive ideals of raunch culture. Figure 5.1 shows how she appeared in the January 2000 "Naked Supermodel Special!" edition of *GQ*, in which she
posed nude and almost nude. I share this not to "slut-shame" or judge
Ms. Trump. How she finds her place in the world is her business. I am interested, however, in the cultural implications of Melania Trump's modeling career in relation to her position as first lady. Can we imagine the
backlash Hillary Clinton of the earnest 1990s hair bands or Laura Bush
in the tidy sweater sets might have faced for modeling naked? Michelle

Obama could not even wear sleeveless tops without being criticized for the "high crime" of displaying her biceps. That Melania, and by association Donald, received little pushback for the *GQ* series of naked photos during his candidacy suggests that the values of raunch culture—e.g., the best women are hot babes—have been widely assimilated.

#babes4Trump—the Sexualization of Politics

The US porn nation, in its ever-expansive capacity to sexualize *everything*, is also visible in partisan politics. For example, some of Trump's supporters explicitly link provocative female bodies with Trump paraphernalia in their social media feeds. Timothy noticed what he called a "sexualization of politics" leading up to the 2016 election:

> These accounts that post these photos of women, they always have Trump stickers on these coolers, or they're always flying the Trump flag while they're at the beach and so there's this weird sexualization of politics, too. So for example, I saw #babes4Trump, a trending thing where women were at the beach in bikinis or thongs and they would have a Trump flag around their back and their butt showing.

Angelina shared, "I've noticed some women on my Instagram feed posing with the 'Make America Great Again' flags and hats dressed in short shorts, flannel tops with crop tops and exposed cleavage as well as cowboy boots." Images similar to those described by Angelina and Timothy appeared in a July 2017 article on TeaParty.org (see figure 5.2). The headline reads "MAGA (Make America Great Again) Bikinis Multiply!" and continues, "Don't hate them because they are beautiful. With summer in full swing, gorgeous women who call themselves Babes for Trump are flaunting their bangin' bikini bodies on social media."[23] There are also a number of memes, like those in figure 5.3, that contrast "sexy" conservative women with "ugly, unfeminine" liberal ones.

FIGURE 5.2A-B. From the Twitter account #babes4trump. Source: Twitter

FIGURE 5.3A-B. "Sexy" conservative women vs. "Ugly" liberal women. Source: Reddit

Raunch culture is not confined to Trump supporters—people of any political leaning may promote the sexist value of pornified femininity. What is significant about these images, and dozens more you can find with a single search, is the wedding of conservative politics with "bangin' bikini bodies," a new development in the party of traditional values.

Timothy saw the #babes4trump phenomenon as a reaction to progressive women and the women's marches. He said:

> It was like this backlash towards feminists who were uniting against Trump. It was this women's movement to say, "Well we're women and we're for Trump," and had this weird sexual dimension. I've never seen this combination of sexual objectification and political campaigning with any previous candidate on either side of the aisle before.

Some conservatives belittled the marchers' looks, as Jody, who is white and 18, discussed in her interview:

> I went to the women's march in Lexington. I didn't even post on Facebook that I went, like I posted pictures on Snapchat of my posters and nothing else, but I saw a lot of other people's opinions about the women's march. I heard mostly other women sharing that one meme, "Trump, in his first day of office got more fat women marching than Michelle Obama ever did" or whatever. First of all, fuck that. Second of all, what that meme is saying is "let's ignore the 2.4 million women marching around the globe because some of them were probably ugly." The meme negated everything they were trying to say with that march by using misogyny, if that isn't the most ironic thing I've ever heard.

Name-calling women who critique sexism as "fat" and "ugly" is a time-worn strategy for dismissing feminist thought and activism, but posing conservative women as hot with "bangin' bikini bodies" is new. No longer are misogynists confined to the old dichotomy framing women as virgins or whores. Raunch culture has facilitated a new sexist dichot-omy: *hot or not*. Even conservative Christians have their own twist on the hot trope—"modest is hottest."[24]

Conservative Christians in the Age of Trump

As I write this on July 12, 2019, poll tracker FiveThirtyEight finds that 42.4% of Americans approve of Trump's job performance. His job approval is consistently higher among Republicans (79%), especially conservative Republicans (84%) and evangelical Protestants (68%).[25] The support of this last group—conservative Christians—is especially puzzling to quite a few experts, and the topic of many think pieces.[26] Several people I interviewed specifically discussed this, like Kevin, who is 43 and white:

> It's fascinating to me that they were accepting of this guy who's a pag-eant owner and has had multiple allegations of assault and who has been twice divorced and on his third marriage, and his most recent one has posed for a lot of photos that would be identified as raunch culture. To be able to just discount all of that, I'm dumbfounded. Especially when you look at the voices who have come out in support, and are so willing to compromise their values, and compromise the things their predecessors would have never done. The pulpits have been scandalously silent on that behavior, which is fascinating too.

On the one hand, it's not surprising that 81% of "white, born-again, evan-gelical Christians" voted for Trump since this demographic consistently votes Republican: 78% of white evangelicals voted for Bush in 2004, 74% for McCain in 2008, and 78% for Romney in 2012.[27] On the other, it is surprising that Trump received a higher percentage of white evangeli-cal votes than previous, more devout Republican candidates, including George W. Bush, and that he received these votes despite being such a poor representative of Christian family values.

After pornography star Stormy Daniels revealed that she had had an affair with Donald Trump, a new flurry of articles emerged querying why white evangelicals, "who loudly proclaim their devotion to the teachings of the Bible, continue to support the thrice-married, six-times-bankrupted, multiple-times-unfaithful, chronically lying president."[28] Frances FitzGerald, author of *The Evangelicals*, found that many conservative evangelicals who voted for Trump were affiliated with the Tea Party, and cared more about small government, job creation, and deporting illegal immigrants than Trump's Christian credentials.[29] Some conservative Christian leaders are silent on or tolerant of Trump's lecherous behavior because they, and their parishioners, are single-mindedly focused on limiting abortion rights and voted in hopes of a conservative Supreme Court pick that might tilt the court to overturn *Roe v. Wade*, something that Trump rewarded them with by nominating Brett Kavanaugh. A 2018 sociological study of Trump voters identified Christian nationalism as a key factor explaining why some Christians support Trump.[30] Christian nationalists describe themselves as "adher[ing] to a political platform that advocates for Christian principles in government and law."[31]

Again, what has not been explored concerning conservative Christian support for Trump is raunch culture. Timothy, quoted earlier, who recently finished seminary and had just been named pastor of a Methodist church in Southeast Kentucky, said that he had observed elements of raunch culture "leaking in" to evangelical circles for some time. He elaborated:

> In evangelical churches, I've seen raunch culture leaking in and baptized as long as it's in the confinements of a heterosexual marriage. You can say vulgar things like, "My smokin' hot wife," or, "God gave me this beautiful woman." It's this weird sexualization from the pulpit of evangelical women as long as it's within the confines of a heterosexual marriage. And then there's sermon series that I've noticed that are geared towards college students about sex that mirror raunch culture but making it Christian,

you know? Like, "It's okay to give blow jobs" and things like that. I've even heard pastors talk about oral sex, describing it, as long as you're married. It's like they're trying to get people excited or aroused, but only if they do it "God's way" instead of outside of that. I find the same amount of vulgarity in that as I would if it were secular.

Timothy's observations align with the work of historian Dagmar Herzog, who has researched sexual changes in conservative Christian culture. Since the mid-1970s, Herzog found, "evangelical Christians have been pushing the good word that evangelicals have more fun—that godly sex is the most fabulous sex."[32] Herzog describes an evangelical sex industry of self-help and sex advice books and columns, some of which offer readers "their own brand of Christian porn," of lurid stories of "sexual sin" followed by tales of repentance and forgiveness. Sociologist Kelsy Burke updated Herzog's work on conservative Christian sexuality, exploring how Christians use digital media to improve their sex lives.[33] In other words, enter stage right the internet—harbinger of raunch culture. Burke found a wealth of sex advice and support for "sanctioned"— married heterosexual—couples on sites like BetweenTheSheets.com and LustyChristianLadies.com (400,000 hits in one month, for example).

Julia, who is white, 46, and a professor at a conservative seminary, also brought up the trend of pastors discussing their "hot wives." She said, "I think it's their attempt to build up their women and build up sexuality, which is not bad in itself, to move away from 'sex is dirty, save it for the one you love,' but why do youth pastor's wives have to be hot?" As previously noted, "being hot" is compulsory for women in raunch culture no matter how religious, how old, or how uninterested any woman is in attaining this goal. Charlotte, Timothy's wife, who is white and 23, also noticed raunch infiltrating worship on her college campus and shared the following story:

It was 2014 and the Baptist Campus Ministries had Greek Tuesday Night Live and invited the pastor from whatever that awful low-church gimmicky mega-church is in [college town]. He preached the expected hellfire/Greeks repent sermon, which made me upset because in no way was his approach productive. The kicker was instead of a nice pleasant benediction he leaves the stage in his skinny jeans and tight-fitting shirt with, "If you'll excuse me, I'm going to go home and have sex with my smokin' hot wife."

Charlotte concluded she thought it was his "weird desperate way to seem relatable." In the 2020s, I expect there is little more "relatable" to young evangelical Christians than raunch culture.

I asked Timothy if female pastors talked about their husbands in similar terms, i.e., "my smokin' hot husband." He responded that he had never heard women talk about men that way from the pulpit, explaining that "homophobia" was why this would not be acceptable. He said, "First of all, a woman probably wouldn't be preaching at one of those circles, but if she did, and were to say something about how hot her husband was, or things like, 'He's been working out' or, 'Look at his muscles,' it would probably be perceived differently because of the homophobic underlying mechanisms within the audience." I asked Timothy to elaborate on how a heterosexual woman discussing her husband's desirability connected to homophobia. He said, "They don't want to picture their pastor, the male, as a sexual object, but it's okay if it's his wife." He continued,

> There is an underlying fear that it's homoerotic if we think about a male pastor in a sexual way. It conjures up the fantasy of a sexualized male. I think there's this fear of sexualizing men, besides just seeing them as people that have sexual urges or desires. They don't want to make the male a sexual object to lust after. At least, in the gatherings that include both genders. I've never been in an exclusively female evangelical gathering, but that seems to be the tone or the mood from what I can gather.

The sexist double standard of raunch culture is clearly visible in Timothy's example here. The evangelicals he described approve the sexual objectification of women within the confines of a "godly" marriage, but are uncomfortable with the sexual objectification of men. Further, this is not because objectification itself is bad or "sinful," but because envisioning a man as an object opens the door to homoeroticism. Notice here, in this hypothetical scenario, all the actors, all the subjects, all the ones whose opinions matter, are men. Conservative Christian and raunch cultures work well in unison because both systems position women as inferior to men, and both seek to control women's sexual expression.

Emboldening Chauvinists: "Grab 'Em by the Pussy"

I was thinking about the horrible things he was saying on the bus with Billy Bush that were being recorded and played on national news. I probably heard that story 50 times. I thought, "It's over, he might as well hang it up." And then what happened? Billy gets fired and Trump gets elected president. How do you even wrap your head around that?
—Susan, 58, white

In October 2016, a month before the presidential election, the *Washington Post* released a 2005 recording of Donald Trump speaking with entertainment host Billy Bush about sexually assaulting women. They were riding in an *Access Hollywood* bus to the set of *Days of Our Lives*, on which Trump was scheduled to appear. While watching a feed of the approaching location on the bus, Trump and Bush noticed Arianne Zucker, the actress waiting to escort Trump to the show set. Trump made the following comment: "I've got to use some Tic Tacs in case I start kissing her. You know, I'm automatically attracted to beautiful—I just start kissing them. It's like a magnet. Just kiss. I don't even wait. And when you're a star, they let you do it. You can do anything. Grab 'em by the pussy. You can do anything."[34] While the reaction of public officials from both sides of the aisle was swift and condemning, Trump remained in the race and, as we know, became president. So why wasn't the "grab 'em by the pussy" comment a deal breaker for the highest office in the US? I argue it is partly because raunch culture normalized the sexual objectification of women while e-bile habituated internet users to uncivil discourse, in particular, degrading, offensive, and bullying language toward minority members.

Since Trump's election, there has been much written about how the unexpected outcome has "emboldened" people to express sexist and racist attitudes. Ten percent of those I interviewed discussed incidents of sexual assault, like Kassidy, who is white and 21:

> Men will literally come up and try to grab you. It's happened to me twice. It was downtown Lexington. "If the president can do it, so can I." I'm like, "Absolutely not, I'll break your fucking arm and I'll break his fucking arm." If he tries to grab my pussy, you'll come away with broken bones. It is absolutely ridiculous the things that have been tolerated, permitted, and allowed because we're seen as less. What is the president's job? To make us safer, to make us feel comfortable. I don't feel any of those things on a state level, local level, international level especially. It's absolutely ridiculous.

Gwen, who is white and 23, also spoke about observing a sexist trickle-down Trump effect in some men's behavior:

> People find it more acceptable just to say whatever the fuck they want. Like the pussy-grabbing comment. Do you know how many men I've heard non-ironically say that stuff now? Do you know how many men I've heard say that before? None. Not once have I heard them say something along the lines of, joking or not, "I'll just take what I want." That dominant-man culture has become more of a thing now too. Also, it's six months in and I've noticed, "Why does every man suddenly want to put me in a headlock the first time we have sex?" It frustrates me so bad. Our society has regressed in a bad kind of sexual way, stuff like this, where

we're objectified, so when he says stuff like, "I'll just grab them by the pussy," we are faceless holes without a heart or any brains.

Since Trump gained office, a variety of organizations and individuals have documented a rise in the physical and sexual abuse of child immigrants,[35] an increase in hate crimes on college campuses,[36] greater hate violence directed toward South Asian, Muslim, Sikh, Hindu, Middle Eastern, and Arab communities in the US,[37] a rise in the number of hate groups and participation in those groups,[38] and an increase in the sexual harassment of girls and women in both primary and secondary schools.[39] In 2018, the FBI reported that hate crimes increased for the third year in a row.[40] In addition to seeing more examples of terrible hate crimes, like the October 2018 Pittsburgh shooting in which an anti-Semite murdered 11 Jewish people at the Tree of Life synagogue, I also see an uptick in openly expressed bigotry in social media. At least once a week when I open Facebook, I find a disturbing video of a white person screaming obscenities at a person of color, and/or a man harassing a woman in my feed. Andrew, who is white and 24, observed this:

> I think since Trump became president, it's been more vocally acceptable—
> like all these people who I think were secretly voting for Trump, now
> that he's president they can be more vocal about it. Like, "The rest of the
> country agreed with me, so it's cool for me to be vocal about these shitty
> things that I say." They say, "Oh I'm in the majority, I can say these things."
> And there is no repercussion.

A 2019 Pew poll finds that 65% of Americans "say it's now more common for people to express racist or racially insensitive views; more than four-in-ten say it's more acceptable"[41] than before Trump took office. I googled "racist tirade by a white person" on July 11, 2019, to see how many viral videos of racists were on the web. There were over 50,000 results, and I stopped counting after finding 50 separate videos dated

2016 and later. This overt chauvinism is especially visible now because the combined new technologies of smartphones and social media allow bigoted rants to reach a wider audience.

Mike, who is white, 64, and a political scientist, believes that some liberals, like myself, were blindsided by the 2016 election outcome because "people tend to see chauvinism as being more superficial than it is." Echoing Hillary Clinton in her "basket of deplorables" speech, as well as other political scientists, Mike estimated that 50% of Trump supporters, 18% of all Americans, are racists.[42] Mike believes that key to understanding chauvinism lies in how chauvinists understand personal "freedom."[43] He elaborated:

> If you listen to discourse on race, racists view the ability to impose themselves on black people as a basic requirement of freedom. So you see the videos [personally recorded and uploaded to YouTube and Facebook] of white people causing racial incidents, booting kids out of school, booting kids out of aquarium gift shops, harassing black people in cookouts or walking down the street or taking shelter from the rain. What's interesting to me is that there comes a point where they know they're being filmed and they know it's a good chance of it going viral. And you can see them being determined to carry through. That they're not going to be constrained, they're not going to be stopped. The key thing here is that if you have an expectation of male dominance or you have an expectation of white dominance, you don't feel yourself as a full person unless you're dominant. So you're not really free unless you can act like the racist you are.
>
> People in the videos [of racist tirades] are saying that Trump got elected, so we're in charge now. It's our time. Once again it's, "We've been constrained for so long, we've been targeted for so long. We've been prevented from acting on our beliefs." Then there's a counter-rhetoric—"Go back to your hole, we don't want to hear you, shut up, go away, go back to 4chan"—directed at MRAs and racists and Nazis. But then, on the other hand, if you're from the other perspective, the fact that you're limited only

to 4chan is extremely restraining. You want to be an out racist as opposed to closeted racist.

Christina, who is Latinx and 26, said, "Racist white people have balls now." She explained that she feels both more vigilant and afraid since Trump became president:

> He gave the racists the courage to go up to a black person, go up to a Latina and yell racist slurs at them, punch them, call the police on them. You see it every day. One good example of this: I am in Philly, there's a town in Port Richmond, and it's known to be a very racist neighborhood. Addie [Christina's fiancée] was getting her hair done there, and I was like, "Hey, I'm hungry, I'm going to find a place to eat." And while I was walking I saw a lot of white people, and I was so afraid that I texted Addie, "I just want to text you because I'm the only Latina girl walking down the street." I don't want to attract attention. I don't want an angry old white guy to call the police on me and I get shot or beat up or whatever just because I'm going to find some food. I told her I had made it to the deli and I'm coming back, "Can you please text me or can you please talk to me?" So, definitely my behavior has changed a little bit. Especially in situations like that, because I'm afraid. I'm always smiling. I'm always making eye contact, or not eye contact. I always smile, and say hello if someone says hello to me. Just so I don't give someone a reason to call the cops or start harassing me.

Although racism and sexism are interrelated—those who are racist also tend to be sexist, homophobic, and authoritarian—racism and sexism take different forms.[44] People more easily segregate by race than by sex. In other words, white racists can more easily avoid personal interactions with people of color than male chauvinists can with women. This is because most families and communities include men *and* women.

Patriarchy distinguishes "good" from "bad" women through ideologies like "benevolent sexism."[45] Under benevolent sexism, women who embrace traditional gender roles and reproduce male supremacist dogma merit chivalrous protection. In contrast, those cast as "bad"—feminist, agnostic, Clinton supporters, single, childfree, etc.—*deserve* to be harassed and assaulted. Benevolent sexism "helps to pacify women's resistance to societal gender inequality" as girls and women watch and internalize the stark differences between the ways people treat "virtuous" as opposed to "slutty" females.[46] Of course, no matter how well a girl or woman adheres to patriarchal ideas that detail how to be a good daughter, wife, or mother, men may still harass, abuse, and assault her, and blame her for it.

Hillary Rodham Clinton

It was really hard as a woman to go through and see it happen. Especially because Hillary was a perfectly qualified candidate. Things keep falling apart now that he's in office. There's no silver lining. It's really troubling for women and only going to limit them from breaking past raunch culture having a leader like that and knowing someone like that can get elected. You think of the "grabbing the pussy" scandal, and see that someone who says that can be president but someone who has worked in the field for decades and wanted the job so bad can't be president. It feels really unfair to girls.
—Alexis, 20, white college student

Donald Trump's election to the US presidency demonstrates that harassing and assaulting women is not important enough to disqualify someone from the highest office in the country. It's just "boys being boys" and "locker room talk," in other words, the "natural" order of gender relations in which women's bodies exist for men's pleasure, and women themselves should only speak in ways that support the patriarchal status quo, unlike Hillary Clinton, who dared to believe she could lead. Over her years in politics, especially during her runs for president in 2008 and 2016, Hillary Clinton endured an avalanche of sexist attacks.[47] Watching coverage of 2016 campaign rallies in which Trump encourages supporters to chant "lock her up" is unnerving.[48] Worse and even more disturbing, as late as October 2018, *after* the Manafort and Cohen indictments implicating Trump in attempting to corruptly influence the election, Trump was *still* having rallies and *still* egging on crowds to chant, "Lock her up!" As Jason, observed, "This is what we get when we have all the bullies who got their way throughout life getting their way now. They're perpetuating being an asshole and reveling in it. There's a mob mentality where you see a president having a rally every month. Nobody does that." Seeing a woman so relentlessly pilloried in public sends a chilling message to girls and women: *don't speak out, don't have opinions, and don't imagine yourself leaders of men and women.*

As I digested Clinton's unanticipated loss in November 2016, I turned to the books of Starhawk, the activist, Wiccan, ecofeminist visionary, for comfort and guidance. In her 1993 novel *The Fifth Sacred Thing*, Starhawk writes a spellbinding story exploring how a group of creative people manage to resist a large military force by inviting their would-be captors to *join* rather than conquer them. The plot of the almost 500-page novel overflows with gripping twists. I've taught it several times in gender classes, and we always spend some time exploring the concept of the "Good and Bad Reality." The character Maya explains that the Good Reality and the Bad Reality vie with each other: "In the Good Reality you have a mild headache; in the Bad Reality you have a fatal brain disease. . . . We walk in the Good Reality as if we were treading the thin skin on warm milk. It's always possible to break through and drown."[49]

On November 9, 2016, I woke, like many others, into the Bad Reality. Americans chose a racist, fascist, sexual predator with the vocabulary of a ten-year-old over the most qualified person to ever run for president. Even my body rejected the outcome: I couldn't sleep, I had no appetite, and my stomach was in knots for days. I thought often of Starhawk's words of hope to those trapped in the Bad Reality: "Even in *El Mundo*

Malo [the bad world], the Good Reality is always just on the other surface of things. If you can learn to reach and pull yourself through, you can make miracles."[50] As the giant fascist shadow of a Trump administration darkens my country, I remind myself that the Good Reality is nearby, just beyond the thin surface of now. Hillary Clinton's historic campaign for president put women's agency front and center in the public eye, and her loss to an unashamed chauvinist has helped spawn a new wave of the women's liberation movement.

An effective three-pronged siege, internet porn and raunch culture inure viewers to sexually graphic representations of women while e-bile normalizes online and IRL (in real life) hate speech, a combination that I believe helped usher in the Trump administration. When it is *normal* to see women attacked for speaking out, *normal* to watch men degrade women in pornography, *normal* to see naked women in advertisements, *normal* for women to put up with hearing a steady stream of sexist patter, *normal* for women to fend off unwanted touching from men, *normal* to blame women for the sexual assaults they endure, *normal* to see young women posting sexy selfies, *normal* for boys and men to send unsolicited dick pics, and *normal* to excuse the sexist misconduct of famous people, a politician's sexist speech and behaviors are simply normal to many. Hillary Clinton is, arguably, the antithesis of raunch culture. Where raunch is vapid, HRC is focused and intelligent; where raunch is sex-obsessed and flashy, HRC is direct and administrative; where raunch is narcissistic, HRC is other-directed. Donald Trump embodies raunch culture, and that is how the new sexism of raunch culture helped Donald Trump become president of the United States.

6

Transforming Raunch Culture

Two thousand seventeen began with the Women's March and an estimated 3–5 million marchers in the US and over 7 million people across the globe voicing their support of women's rights. The year continued with people participating in forms of widespread activism—protests, petitions, marches, and phone calls—not seen since the 1960s. That year social media facilitated the #metoo and Time's Up campaigns to stop sexual harassment and assault. For a few days, my Facebook feed was little but "#metoo" posts as women participated in a national conversation about unwanted sexual advances from men. Americans watched as powerful men including Harvey Weinstein, Bill O'Reilly, Les Moonves, Matt Lauer, and Jeffrey Epstein (among some 200-plus others) lost their jobs and faced public censure and/or prison for their harassing and criminal behavior toward women, although Donald Trump remained in office and some, like Brett Kavanaugh, seemed immune from negative consequences for their actions.

In this fertile period of increased gender consciousness, of public conversations about toxic masculinity and subordinated femininity, this chapter asks and answers: how can we transform raunch culture? If, as Angelina argued, "the combination of raunch culture and the new tech age has resulted in women's bodies being viewed as accessible objects," what might change girls and women from objects to subjects in people's eyes? I asked those I interviewed to reflect upon this and together we developed a set of guidelines for a new cultural paradigm. Transformation starts with first *perceiving* the harmful effects of raunch culture, followed by challenging it, mentoring young people in gender equality, advancing a gender studies agenda, providing a pleasure-centered sexual education, and empowering women.

Seeing Raunch Culture: "It's Highjacking Our Lives without Us Even Knowing"

I've heard it so many times, it's comical. I'm chatting with someone—a friend, an acquaintance, a neighbor, a colleague—about my project on raunch culture. I receive a polite smile, a blank look, followed by a flicker of indecision, and then most say, "Oh, how interesting." "Do you know what raunch culture is?" I ask helpfully, and 98% of people do not. Recognition of raunch culture suffers, as I wrote earlier, from the condition of inarticulation. Most people do not have words to describe the hypersexualized images, speech, and attitudes of contemporary culture. Then, without language to quickly convey small and large concepts, communication can be laborious and confusing, perhaps more work than it is worth, especially if others consider the ideas one is expressing controversial. So part of making raunch culture visible entails circulating words that name the phenomenon.

Linguists have long known that language influences how we perceive social life.[1] For example, consider the phrases "racial profiling" and "sexual harassment." Both these concepts entered into public use in the past 30–40 years. Did racial profiling and sexual harassment exist before people named these practices, and critiqued the abuse? Of course! Racial profiling was simply life as a racial minority, and sexual harassment what a woman expected without a male escort (and sometimes *from* the one supposedly "protecting" her). The new words facilitate awareness and the *possibility* of change. Dylan, who is white and 28, specifically discussed this. He said that raunch culture "has to be visible" before we can dismantle it:

> It's super invisible for people who have the untrained eyes. People need to know it exists, how it harms people, and they need to know how it could possibly affect issues in our society. To be honest, a lot of those people probably wouldn't care anyway. But the more you make it visible, or are critical of it, and look at how it's affecting people, then the tide of history starts to ebb and flow and it may help.

Kayla thinks that it is difficult for young people to see raunch culture because "there's no contrast. It's highjacking our lives without us even knowing." She explained, "If everything in a room is gray, then how can you tell the difference between this gray item and that one. It should be glaringly obvious how awful these things are, but because it's just what is, people don't have anything to compare it to." Millennials and those in Generation Z urgently need more conversations about raunch culture because, as previously explored, hypersexualization *is* culture for them. In an image-based digital culture, the average consumer sees up to 10,000 advertisements a day, switches between screens up to 21 times an hour, and has an attention span of eight seconds.[2] Westerners thus encounter a smorgasbord of pouty female faces and provocatively arranged female bodies in many places: the grocery checkout, on billboards, on buses, really anywhere there is ad space. Those on social media see sexy pictures of women and girls scrolling through their feeds. Embedded in many of these images are the values of raunch culture: women's bodies are consumable.

Since children see this very specific raunch beauty ideal from the moment they begin looking at screens (which may be as young as two years old),[3] Rebecca, who is white and 25, wondered how the images unconsciously affect consumers. She said,

> I don't even notice it, because I just see it everywhere. You're inundated with this all the time. How do you change what your subconscious is telling you? My subconscious is saying women who look a certain way and behave a certain way are the epitome of femininity. How do I say that I don't believe that anymore? You have to decide to value something else other than that.

Thus, the first way to begin transforming raunch culture is to circulate words that allow people to perceive, name, and discuss it, words that logically dismantle the gender inequality on display, and empower people to express their support for the bodily autonomy of all people.

Challenging Raunch Culture: "This Isn't Right!"

Jordan, who is white and 20, said that it is important that people both see raunch culture and recognize that it "isn't right!" She explained:

> I think first of all people need to accept that it's a real issue, it's a real thing, because I think a lot people are in denial of it. There's too many people that are like, "Oh you're just being weird, there's nothing wrong with this," and it's everywhere. I think the first step is people actually admitting, "Oh, hey, this isn't right." And then from there starting to stand up like, "Hey, we're not going to watch this if you do this. We're not going to put up with you checking out every single girl and talking about her body under your breath and telling your friends. That's not okay." So just getting more people to just stand up, and say that it's an actual problem.

Confronting others about their participation in and promotion of raunch culture is difficult to do. We want to get along with one another and not rock the boat. We don't want to stand out as different, nor make others feel uncomfortable. It's also just risky. Those who critique oppressive cultural practices chance drawing an unpleasant, defensive response. Stephanie, who is black and 50, spoke about this at length:

> Women who speak out against raunch culture are highly targeted: "Slut, you're lying." Not necessarily in those words, but there is this deep-seated desire to hide this. "You bitch, shut up." There will be some type of examination on the way she looks. If she is not considered attractive or appealing by conventional patriarchal standards, every "flaw," every pock on her skin, her face, her body, her buttocks will be laid open for brutal condemnation. If she were the opposite—a woman who is desirable physically but nonetheless through her criticism of raunch culture has made herself known to be averse to it—they may not talk about pocked skin or small breasts or full tummy. What they will then do is try to degrade her

in terms of her sexual self, then she's a slut. Still she is degraded, she is degraded physically on both ends.

We see these kinds of attacks on women who challenge sexism—or even just dare to lead like Nancy Pelosi and Alexandria Ocasio-Cortez—online, in the media, and face-to-face. The misogynist rantings of media personalities like Rush Limbaugh and Sean Hannity, along with the casual, brutal sexual objectification of women from shock jocks like Howard Stern, illustrate this dynamic. Patriarchy perpetuates itself partly by widely disseminating language that "degrades" and demonizes those who oppose oppression.[4]

But it is possible to introduce critical awareness about raunch culture in ways that strengthen relationships and make them more rewarding. For example, Valerie, who is 21 and biracial, and Elizabeth, who is white and 20, support each other in their feminist awareness and actively surround themselves with people who are open to conversations about inequality. Longtime close friends, Valerie and Elizabeth have spent hundreds of hours discussing feminist issues like raunch culture, and actively advocate progressive ideas and policies. Valerie explained, "We constantly point it out. We don't let things slide." Elizabeth offered an example: "If they make little sexist jokes, we'll be like, 'That's not funny.' We won't laugh at it. We don't condone it." It helps that both Valerie and Elizabeth have supportive parents who welcome their insights on the culture and encourage them to "stand up" for their beliefs, as Valerie's father said after she went on one of her many rants about the "ridiculous way women are treated." They are also impatient with those who think raunch culture is inevitable. Valerie explained, "I don't like it when people don't think it can be changed. Everybody expects society to be this way so they won't attempt to change it. They're afraid to point out that it's not okay because the rest of society expects it to be that way." Elizabeth observed, "Who said it's supposed to be this way? We're the ones making it this way."

Lauren, who is white and 39, also believed that it is important to confront people when they are sexist rather than cut them from one's life, because, as she said, "They're not bad people, they're humans. I think automatically saying, 'You're an asshole, get away from me,' is not going to change anything." Recently single, and trying to meet men on dating apps, Lauren has encountered a lot of obnoxious behavior. During our interview, she grabbed her phone and opened up a text she had just sent a man she had paired with on one of the apps. His first question to her had been: "How big are your tits?" She read me what she wrote him in response:

> Here's the thing, you asked me for my tits before you ask me anything about who I am. Sex is way more about someone's mind than how many handfuls my tits are. I like sex, I like figuring out what a dude likes and am willing to go kinky places, but being treated like a hole to put your dick in is so off-putting. I suspect the internet has done something to how people interact. You're probably not a bad guy. Here's what I like, I like when a man takes instructions. When he hears me say, slow down, he does.

She said she was surprised and pleased that he responded, "Oh, okay," rather than "You're a cunt." Lauren reflected that people don't know things until they've been told:

> I think you have to say, "You're not a bad person. I don't think you're a bad person for subscribing to this. I don't think you've known anything else, but from my perspective this is why it sucks." If you hear a well-reasoned argument then you'll respond, and that was my tactic. But I was also just like, "Come on, I'm a human being."

Some of those I interviewed observed that most people have never analyzed their participation in raunch culture before. Elizabeth explained, "They've never had anyone call them out on it. No one has ever questioned them because that is how it's supposed to be. We try to be the people in their lives that are like, 'But that's not right, you can't say stuff like that.'" Angelina agreed: "If we let people around us continue to spew hatred then they'll never be forced to think about their language and potentially stop participating in it." The more such challenges are institutionally instigated and supported, like by the Gillette razor advertisement critiquing toxic masculinity or Barack Obama, who, when discussing men and masculinity, said, "If you are confident about your strength, you don't need to show me by putting somebody else down. Show me how strong you are that you can lift somebody else up,"[5] the easier it is for individuals to challenge daily experiences of sexism.

Tips for Talking about Raunch Culture

So how *does* one talk about raunch culture without being dismissed as a "feminist killjoy," as Jordan quipped? While folks tend to *see* sexualization pretty quickly with a few examples, understanding the multifaceted impact of raunch culture typically takes about 45 minutes of focused conversation for those unfamiliar with the concept. Because you likely won't be in charge of a class or an interview, this may mean initiating several conversations on the topic at different times with different points of entry—perhaps Instagram one day, girls' clothing another time, unsolicited dick pics when women complain about them, and college party themes like "CEOs and Office 'Hos" later. Considering your own participation in raunch culture, if you are a young woman who enjoys dressing up in stripper heels and going to college parties, or if you are a young man who "gets horny" scrolling through your Instagram feed as Tom shared, let yourself off the hook. You can still acknowledge the negative consequences of raunch culture—that it supports rape culture, privileges materialism and porn star beauty over human connections, encourages toxic masculinity, and represents women as compliant sex dolls—without beating yourself up.

If you are new to this kind of conversation, I recommend first discussing raunch culture with those you think will be receptive to your perspective. If possible, keep the dialogue focused on critiquing the structure of pornification and minimize all illustrations of personal behavior. Remind folks that we are all shaped by social norms and participate in practices that sometimes cause harm in spite of our best intentions, whether it is the Nike sneakers we buy, our environmental footprint, or the porn we watch. If you find yourself getting emotional, in particular, angry and defensive, by what you perceive to be another's unwillingness, or inability, to see and acknowledge the inequality that is so obvious to you, take a deep breath and pause the discussion. Take control in a gentle way, saying something like, "I appreciate how you are engaging with these ideas. I think I'm not explaining myself the best right now. Let's talk it about it later." And then change the subject to something neutral. Mentally bookmark the topic and, the very next time it is relevant, bring up the ideas again in the new context with a positive mindset. Your attitude will be fresh and you will likely have different ways to convey your thoughts that may be more effective. This is a good strategy to use when introducing someone to any paradigm-challenging idea—not only raunch culture, but also white privilege, climate change, or income inequality.

I did this at a family reunion in June 2018 when chatting with my 28-year-old cousin, Christopher. We were discussing feminism and the #metoo movement when Christopher casually disparaged TERFs (trans-exclusionary radical feminists).[6] This rubbed me the wrong way because I believe the term "TERF" does a disservice, and is harmful, to people's understanding of the revolutionary potential of radical feminism. I tried to explain this, found myself getting testy with how complicated it was to swiftly describe, and then changed the subject. I knew Christopher was a feminist and I was not angry with him. I felt frustrated with the ways those who seek to maintain systems of domination use language to misrepresent feminism, especially radical feminism, which is more often demonized than any other feminist perspective. I had mentally bookmarked the discussion and, 30 minutes later, seized the opportunity to better explain my objection to Christopher. Both of us are avid fans of the adaptation of *The Handmaid's Tale* on Hulu. While we were discussing some of the plot points, I said, "*The Handmaid's Tale* is a radical feminist story. It explores and centers gender, and we need stories that do this. Radical feminism is much bigger than the very few folks who are TERFs. When folks trash TERFs, I am concerned that it ends up undermining the important work of radical feminism, so you might want to think twice about using that term."

Outgrowing Raunch Culture

I started this project struggling with 20 years of accumulated anger and frustration with sexist media representations, and feeling pessimistic about the end of raunch culture. I asked the people I interviewed to consider how we might transform raunch, while secretly thinking it was impossible. I was unable to perceive how to change the sexualization of culture absent an apocalyptic event eliminating the internet, and that did not strike me as a future scenario to root for. It was only when I interviewed Emily, who is black and 23, that I had my first surge of real hope that raunch had an expiration date, if not culturewide, at least in the minds and hearts of individuals.

Emily had shared a fairly commonplace story: she'd been partying with some friends at a local college bar, which she described as a "hookup scene" and, after explaining that she had a boyfriend, found herself in a "friend-zone" conversation with a slightly drunken young man who was systematically evaluating all the women in his immediate purview. He pointed at one, then another, and said to Emily in a running commentary, "I could take her home. Nah, I don't want her. I could bang her." Emily explained that she was not bothered by his interest in meeting a woman—that was to be expected at a bar full of young singles on a Friday night—but by how he talked about the women: as pieces of ass he could choose between. She was "dumbfounded" by his attitude, and uneasily wondered how many men had said similar things about her. As we talked about transforming raunch culture, I brought up the young man she had met out that night, asking her what she thought might change *his* attitudes about women. Emily responded:

> I feel like he really needs someone to break his heart. That sounds bad, but he needs to be humbled. He needs to understand the value of women, that we're not here so you can just bang us for a night, and forget about us, and not talk to us. We're loving creatures, we're nurturing creatures. He obviously needs that. He needs some kind of nurturing, some kind of love, and not just a one-night stand, because he's not going to be satisfied. He doesn't seem like he's satisfied, 'cause he's picking and choosing like a gumball machine. Or like a vending machine. It's like, "I want a Sprite today." Building an actual relationship, whether it's a friendship or dating relationship, I feel like that's so much more important than just hooking up with people.

Emily also narrated the journey her brother "Jeffrey" had taken through raunch culture. She described her brother as "the epitome of a man in raunch culture." Before meeting his current girlfriend, Jeffrey had dated only foreign white women, Russian or Austrian women. "He wanted the fashion end of it, so he wanted a model," Emily shared:

> He always said he wanted foreign white women and it always threw me for a loop. I was like, "This is all you like? Not even Hispanic women, only foreign white women, that's it?" And then he actually tried it out. He went to New York for a couple of months to live with his aunt and met all kinds of foreign white women in New York. He got to meet and be with all these girls and then I guess it kind of wore off. I think he was jaded by raunch culture, so when he finally got it, he was like, "This is cool and all, but it's superficial." He wasn't happy. He'd date one or two for a month, or a month and a half, and he wasn't satisfied. It was just not all

it was cracked up to be. I was like, "I told you to broaden your horizon; you shouldn't just generalize every foreign white woman. You should just say, 'I want a good woman,' and then go from there, because you can't say because of someone's race or someone's job that they're going to be a good fit for you."

Emily credits Jeffrey's new girlfriend with his evolution:

> She's completely different than all the girls he wanted. She's black. She's tall, but not super thin. She played volleyball, but now she just works, she's completely different. He appreciates her way more than he would appreciate one of the models. I listen to the way he talks about her and I was like, "He really does care about her, this is so different."

Emily's description of Jeffrey suggests that some may outgrow the insecure, status-obsessed, peer-pressured, competitive, never-satisfied, superficial, and hierarchical adolescent sensibility of raunch culture in favor of love and authenticity

Mentoring Young People

Several of those I interviewed, like Randall, who is 29 and white, discussed transforming raunch culture by talking about it with their younger siblings and cousins. Randall spends a lot of time with his 20-year-old brother and, when he can, gently tries to guide him away from unconscious sexism. Randall explained,

> He's been exposed to raunch culture his whole life, he was born in 1996. So if it's something that's ingrained in him that he doesn't understand I'll be like, "Hey, that's not the best way to go about that." I just give him a small lesson, but not like I'm higher, like "let me teach you," but just talk with him. Because I know that his family's not, and his friends probably aren't, because they're also 20. So I'm like, "Hey, you know that this

is wrong because" if he uses this language and, "You shouldn't say that because you might not mean for it to be derogatory or sexist or anything but that's the way that it comes off." I try to help him get to that point to not be as influenced by it.

Jason, who is white and 40, said frankly that "men need to be more proactive":

> Acknowledge that it's there, then break it down and explain it to children. It's on men to explain to their sons there should be a level of respect, whether it's turning you on or not, "If there's a woman who's dancing on Instagram that doesn't mean she wants to see your dick. She's doing what she wants to do and that's not an invitation. If you were posting a picture of yourself playing piano and someone started saying that's great, let me see your dick, how would you feel if that's all people wanted from you?" It's on men to explain to their sons that that sort of behavior is wrong. You treat a human being like a human being. I think that's how it matters and can be changed.

During our interview, Kelly, who is white and 21, brought up her 14-year-old sister, who "bragged about being catcalled." Kelly explained that it is important to talk with young people about their real value. She said, "It doesn't matter what's on your face. What matters is what's in your heart. And, are you on fire for something? Because that gives life meaning."

Emily also talked about her teenage sister. She serves as a role model, confidant, and counselor to 15-year-old "Allison." Emily shared that Allison had been through a rough time the past year: "There was a situation where she'd given a boy oral sex and he videotaped it and put it on Instagram. The whole school saw it, other kids from other schools have seen it and she was traumatized." A shy honor student, Allison struggled to handle the damage to her reputation and the subsequent bullying.

Emily shared how she and their family supported Allison during this painful period:

> We've told her if you want people to look at you differently you have to change what you do. You have to excel academically, you have to excel at everything you do because every time they look at you, every time they think about you, they're going to think about this video. You have to give them something more positive to think about when they think about you. So as soon as she did everything started to change for her. She got a really great group of friends, they're all, there are four or five of them and they run track together so they're all really close, really tight, and they have her best interest at heart. They were the kind of friends who stood up for her when people were showing the video and things like that and I was like, "These are the kind of people you need around you, people who are going to build you up and not break you down."

Emily explained that Allison rallied though the ordeal with the help of her family and a whole new set of friends. Several folks, like Makenzie, echoed Emily's tactics for empowering Allison. Makenzie believed that surrounding oneself with like-minded others is a path out of raunch culture. Makenzie said, "Obviously a lot of it is your own work, but knowing people and being with certain people who are supportive is everything!"

Porn Is Not Sex Education

Brian, who is white and 25, considered internet pornography the single greatest contributor to raunch culture. He said, "If you were picking just one thing you could take away and not be here tomorrow and raunch culture would at least be reduced, it would have to be access to the porn." Alexis concurred, "Out of all the things that make raunch culture what it is, pornography and the sex industry have a colossal impact. It has an impact on every young person in today's society." Many passionately advocated for better sex education. For example, Kayla said, "porn has to stop being de facto sex ed!" She continued:

> I think that people of my generation and people younger than me have no understanding of how powerful sex is. And how beautiful it can be and also how horribly destructive it can be. They just wave it around like it's nothing. Just like they make really violent jokes and talk about violent guns. When we see gun violence all the time in movies and on video games, we lose the understanding of how powerful a gun is. I think sex has to be something that people start respecting, and I don't mean from a waspy standpoint like "only have sex in marriage," and stuff like that. That's not what I'm talking about. I'm talking about sex is a powerful thing!

Timothy, who is white, 25, and a pastor, uses radical feminist anti-pornography books to counsel men distressed about watching pornography. He explained, "It's almost like a Stockholm syndrome type of thing, like they hate the fact that they like it, but they like it nonetheless." Timothy found that providing men a feminist context to perceive their pornography use is often transformative:

> I always say, don't give them a Christian devotional if you want somebody to stop watching pornography, just give them a book by Andrea Dworkin. As a Christian I believe that pornography is not God's will for a Christian disciple to do, but I don't think it's because, arbitrarily, God just doesn't like pornography because it's sexual or weird. I think that God would be against pornography because it objectifies and damages women who are involved in the industry, and there's harm that's done to people's sexuality. So I think when people realize why it's unethical or why it's damaging or a negative thing versus just, arbitrarily, "I shouldn't do it, I did it, and now I feel bad and I need to be forgiven and then I'm going to do it again," they realize it's bad because it has this practical impact on people's lives that harm them. I've learned that people seem to struggle less with it or have less of an obsession with it.

Timothy noted a turning point when men realize that "it's not just all about themselves and how they feel after watching it, or how they feel before they watch it, and instead about who they're watching and to what end." When the men he talks with can see that pornography affects the workers, colors their own relationships, fuels negative attitudes about women, and is sexual junk food, Timothy saw real change.

Year after year I poll my students on the content of their "sex ed" programs in their middle and high schools. They roll their eyes and groan, expressing frustration with how little their school systems taught them. Growing up in the Bible Belt, 80% of my students had faith-based abstinence-only sex education programs, like a school assembly featuring a charismatic speaker who frightens students with misinformation about the prevalence of STDs and birth control failures, and then urges them to stay "pure" until they get married. A lucky few learn how to put a condom on a banana. Virtually *no one* gets an education in sexual pleasure, and same-sex sexuality and relationships are completely ignored. Approximately a quarter of the students I have taught over 25 years share that they had good conversations with parents and/or other adult family members about sexual behavior. The rest are mostly on their own, figuring sex out with their peers and with internet pornography.[7] When adults are uncomfortable talking about sexual behavior, and many schools provide only abstinence-based sex educations, it's unsurprising that young people turn to internet pornography to learn about basic anatomy and the how-tos of sex acts. What I wish for young people beginning to experience desire and arousal is a gentler introduction to physical pleasure than gonzo pornography. They deserve a real sexual education taught by experts,[8] and supported by parents, because internet pornography is not a substitute for sex education.[9]

Along with a better sex education, several of those I spoke with advocated for teaching feminism and gender studies in middle and high school. For example, Thomas, who is white and 20, said, "We shouldn't be finding out about raunch culture in college, because by then you're already so invested in it. So I think that if feminism were offered in high school people could learn that, 'Hey, I don't have to do this to be accepted in society.'" Heather, who is white and 22, specifically credited feminism with helping her "emotionally deal with raunch culture through adolescence." Heather had had an outspoken feminist high school history teacher and, she explained, "all these kids did nothing but badger her. It was really brutal how they would treat her." The exchanges over feminism, the terrible way Heather's peers were acting toward a self-identified feminist, piqued her curiosity and, after she searched for information online, feminist blogs and groups offered her tools to critique the pornification of culture.

A Note on Trigger Warnings

Talking about many of the subjects covered in this book has the potential to upset people. This is not only because some may be invested in systems of domination and want to maintain the status quo, but because some may have suffered sexual harassment, abuse, and/or assault. Is it helpful then to offer a trigger warning before discussing dimensions of raunch culture? "Trigger warnings," advance notice that one will be seeing and/or discussing something possibly upsetting that might recall a traumatic experience, are getting much attention these days. For example, in the environment of the academy, psychologist Jonathan Haidt argues that trigger warnings are overprotective because they "coddle" students, and thus inhibit intellectual and emotional growth.[10] Further, too many students opting out of a discussion after a trigger warning can certainly compromise classroom learning. I also think trigger warnings become meaningless if they are overused. In my mind, there is an important difference between seeing a gruesome image and discussing the novel *Mrs. Dalloway*. A recent study also finds that trigger warnings are ineffective: those who received them and those who did not felt similarly after being exposed to disturbing content.[11]

All this acknowledged, I *do* use trigger warnings in the classroom, and sometimes even during one-on-one conversations (along the lines of "Is it okay if we talk about this?"), and will continue doing so. I began using trigger warnings as a new teacher in the 1990s, well before it was trendy or controversial. While I do not offer a trigger warning every day in every class (which I arguably could, considering the material we cover), I do so for violent content, especially when I show pornography. I warn students when I will show them a violent image, and offer them the opportunity to step outside the classroom or simply avert their eyes. Over the years, students have responded differently to seeing explicit material in the classroom. Throughout the 2000s, most students would white-knuckle through it, and stay for the duration. Then there was a period of a few years starting in 2013 when up to half the class would trickle out during the video screening. I planned for this and led a discussion in another classroom about the content with those who walked out while a graduate student stayed with the students still watching the video. In 2016, the students started looking at their phones rather than leaving the classroom when we watched the pornography compilation. This surprised me but I supported, and continue to support, them using their phones like this. I applaud this clever solution they devised. Glancing between their phones and the screen allows everyone to see the visual text while also giving them little breaks from the stress of watching it, and spares the shy ones the embarrassment of leaving. In my experience, providing trigger warnings is a natural part of teaching both sociology and gender studies as it respects and honors the students' individual journeys.

Sisterhood Is Powerful

While I worked on a draft of this chapter, the US Senate confirmed Brett Kavanaugh to the Supreme Court. I sunk briefly back into the dark place I had descended to in the immediate wake of the 2016 election. There was so much at stake with this appointment for minority groups: women's reproductive rights, immigrants' path to citizenship, police violence against people of color, marriage equality, increased corporate power, voter rights, and new laws empowering Christians to discriminate based on religion, just to name those most in my thoughts at the time. Also up for debate was women's believability describing men's sexual assaults.

In renewed distress and despair, I turned to the radical feminist anthology *Sisterhood Is Powerful* to contextualize this newest manifestation of misogyny in the Trump years. Published in 1970, just as the second wave of the women's liberation movement was gaining momentum, *Sisterhood Is Powerful* features essays, poems, and graphics that document women's growing realization that sisters need to prioritize their own freedom. Second wave feminists used the technique of "consciousness-raising"—coming together in small groups to discuss their experiences—to deprogram themselves from patriarchal conditioning. As editor and activist Robin Morgan wrote, "Women's liberation is the first radical movement to base its politics . . . out of concrete personal experiences. We've learned that those experiences are *not* our private hang-ups. They are shared by every woman, and are therefore political."[12] Fifty years later it is rewarding to see women coming together to share their stories in contemporary digital versions of consciousness-raising like #metoo. In this new wave of the women's liberation movement—what some are calling the fourth wave—women are also leading the grassroots resistance to policies enacted by the Trump administration.[13]

The last question I asked the women I interviewed explored their experiences of sisterhood, in other words, times they had seen women supporting women. In my observation, women depend far more on each other for friendship, companionship, emotional support, fun, validation, help, and affection than they do men. The stereotype that women are catty, backbiting, and endlessly jockeying with one another for men's attention masks an important truth: women *already* demonstrate great love for each other. Women *listen* to one another, feed each other, cry together, travel together, give loving feedback, are available when needed, appreciate one another's vulnerability, and care for and about each other. Women do emotional work like listening, talking, validating, and supporting as well as the practical work of cooking, fixing, mending, childcare, and driving.

Women protect and validate each other. Women turn to each other when we are hurting *and* when we want to celebrate our accomplishments. Lauren said, "When I need to be really heard and understood, I go to women."

Those I interviewed spoke at length about their female friends. Alexis, who is white and 20, said, "my two best friends are my complete support system with just being there—sleepovers, talking, and rushing to each other's side." Rebecca appreciated her roommate for reminding her about what is important. She said, "If I get rejected online, it's usually over some silly thing like my looks. Being judged on those things is frustrating, but my roommate reminds me that I don't actually need any of that validation: 'A week ago you were perfectly happy and we were having so much fun hanging out.'" Angelina explained her process of actively supporting women:

> I support women by every day learning how to let go of passing judgments when I hear about a girl who sleeps around a lot or gossip from other friends about another female who has been branded a "skank" or a "bitch." I think that language is unnecessary even if that girl *is* catty, rude, or ditzy. I don't spread gossip or participate in conversations that demean other females. I support my friends by always being there for them and listening to them. My mom has told me before that people have a tendency to flock towards me and "unburden their souls." I have been in many situations where people have told me secrets and caught themselves telling me things about their life and about their struggles. I have always been a listener. Sometimes that is all that people need in their life.

Faye, who is white and 26, thoughtfully described her experience of consciousness-raising first in college, and later on a women's roller derby team. She explained how she changed from seeing other women as competitors to allies:

> I'd like to start by telling how I used to be and how I am now. So back in college anytime I saw another girl my brain immediately went to, "Oh my

god, I hate her." I didn't know who she was, I was just insecure. A lot of that was rooted in my insecurity. I hate who I used to be. I slut-shamed, I did it all. And it was so bad.

I started learning my last semester in college, "You are a shit bag, you cannot be like this." Now that it's years later, anywhere I go I make it a point to talk to women. I play roller derby and that's a big thing. The internet and different places will make it seem like roller derby is catty and everybody is fighting each other and women take their anger out on everybody, but it's the best thing I've ever been involved. There is such a strong bond between everybody because we are all there doing the same thing, which is very empowering. Every time I'm at practice I feel empowered and I feel supported by the women around me, so I take that into my daily life, and I want to make sure that the women I work with, I'll go out of my way to tell them they've done a good job, especially being in a leadership role.

I say it to the men too, but honestly I don't say it as much as I say it to women because I feel like women need more validation. The empowering point is to hear it from someone like, "You are very good at your job." Even if I'm out at a restaurant and I have a waitress that's super good, I make sure to tell her, "You are really fucking good at your job!" That's what I do. I just make it a point to let women know that they're being a good person. I just want to lift the people that are around me. It's mostly women, but I do it to men too.

Cecilia, who is white and 25, also talked about uplifting women. She glowed as she discussed "bragging on" her female friends:

I brag a lot about how I have really good friends who are very supportive and they always make you feel good. I think what's been really good recently is women seeing that there is more than the way we look. I think just how awesome it is to see the strength and the intelligence and doing all these successful things. I see women being very supportive. I see women brag on their friends because we also have a modesty to us and it's good to have someone talk about your accomplishments. I do that all the time. I'll be like, "So they got a 4.0 their first year in grad school," I just think it's important. I think it's like a snowball effect. If you do it, and you see someone else do it, you'll be like, "I need to do that too, let's build each other up."

Women also offer one another an invaluable service when we model independence, self-reliance, and good self-worth. Emily, for example, appreciated following the lead of "independent" women in her life. She said,

> Every woman I know wants to be a working woman. Every woman I know is independent, strong, and wants to have her own life. It's not that they don't want to get married or be in a relationship. They just want to be able to support themselves in the event that they are by themselves, they'll be alright.

I believe the second wave concept of sisterhood—women building up, appreciating, supporting, nurturing, and empowering one another—is key to transforming raunch culture, and dismantling patriarchy. Centering "sisters" does not mean ignoring other forms of inequality. It is instead a mindful commitment that, no matter the attention-grabbing injustice of the moment, women continue to support feminist goals and empower each other.

I also know women can and do hurt each other. Many women, especially white woman, ally themselves with men over other women.[14] Part of women's socialization within patriarchy is to adopt the values of men. This is clearly seen in the androsexist ethos rewarding girls and women who are "one of the guys." Patriarchy also encourages us to single out women for special vitriol. Consider the horrified focus on Lynndie England in 2004, the only woman photographed engaged in torturing prisoners at Abu Ghraib, or the outpouring of donations to unseat Senator Susan Collins when she voted to confirm Kavanaugh in 2018. What might happen if, rather than focus our rage on individual women who succumb to patriarchal brainwashing, we instead reserved our hardest critiques for toxic masculinity? Let's highlight the many male senators who voted for Kavanaugh, and explore the connection between masculinity and violence in prisons, school yards, workplaces, and homes. And then, let's model ways to be better sisters to one another. To do this, we do not need to reinvent the wheel. Feminist theory already provides a map out of raunch culture, and sisterhood is already visible in women's daily interactions if we choose to see it.

Conclusion—Feminism Is the Solution

Researching and writing about raunch culture in the dystopian Trump years has, at times, been a grim task. Still, I see much to be hopeful for. I am hopeful as I see people discuss feminist ideas about bodily autonomy, with the #metoo reckoning, in the grassroots work of progressives to make political change, with the results of the 2018 midterm election creating the most diverse Congress in the history of the United States, the enthusiasm shown for the progressive policies put forward by Alexandria Ocasio-Cortez, the admiration and reverence given to superhero and cultural meme Supreme Court justice Ruth Bader Ginsberg, and the rapid evolution in norms about gender expression. As a culture, we are moving beyond sex/gender binaries of female/male and feminine/masculine. Despite a loud and at times violent backlash, trans and nonbinary people are changing the culture, carving new sex and gender paths, and thus weakening the armor of patriarchy with young people leading the way.

As I write this in April 2020, in the middle of the global Covid-19 quarantine, I am also hopeful that the sudden pause on social life may nudge Americans away from raunch culture. Unsurprisingly, it's still easy to see evidence of raunch in, for example, the swift creation of coronavirus porn[15] and terms like "dickstancing," which describes men sending out dick pics while practicing social distancing. Further,

Pornhub responded to the international lockdown by making premium content free for a month. Data shows that traffic to Pornhub increased 10–20% in March and April 2020.[16] However, I also observe people focusing on art, family time, and good deeds—I see Zoom choral concerts and elaborate chalk-art creations, YouTube lessons from chefs fixing meals out of what's in their cupboards while children bound in and out of the kitchen, stories about healthcare workers rocking out to Journey songs with each patient recovery, universities and companies donating personal protective equipment, and people dancing in unicorn costumes. I am hopeful we are remembering that who we are, and what matters in our lives, encompasses much more than how "hot" we look.

More than anything else, young people make me hopeful. Unfairly maligned as spoiled and entitled, they suffer while the social safety net erodes. In my classrooms, I observe that they are thoughtful and careful how they speak, less interested in materialism than older generations, and more willing to delay gratification. They are fed up with the trolls and "haters," and seek out opportunities to be positive and support one another as Kelly, passionately demonstrated. She said, "We need to be genuine and fight for each other instead of fighting each other. Don't focus on the negative, don't try to change anybody. It's their job to change. Be you, spread love, don't try to fix people."

Millennials and those in Generation Z deserve better than raunch culture. As Timothy thoughtfully explored, raunch culture pits women and men in a zero-sum game in which one person (usually the woman) has to lose so that the other can win. He explained, "Nobody should have to lose from human sexuality, but with raunch culture somebody does have to lose. There has to be this loss of dignity, loss of social status, or loss of personhood. I think that's one of the defining features of raunch culture is the loss or the void of something." We can reject this zero-sum end product of winner/loser in favor of the feminist paradigm of win/win. Feminism, the political, social, and intellectual movement for gender equality and human uplift, rests on three basic beliefs: that patriarchy exists, that greater equality improves social life, and that everyone has the right to bodily autonomy. We all win when feminists win. For example, feminist gains in the workforce improve everyone's work/life balance, feminist victories in climate change legislation protect the globe for all its inhabitants, and feminist initiatives for LGBTQ people foster better relationships between multiple groups—sexual and gender majority and minority members, encompassing women, men, trans, and non-binary people.

The path out of raunch culture must also include envisioning new paradigms, and perhaps Covid-19 is helping Westerners do this. Happiness research finds that the values of raunch culture—fame, status, and money—are directly opposed to those that actually foster happiness— meaningful relationships, engaging work, and feeling connected to something bigger than oneself. We can make individual choices that lessen the grip of raunch by allowing ourselves to be silly and vulnerable, having fun, lightening up, and paying attention to how we feel, not how we look. We can take social media fasts, let ourselves off the hook, appreciate women, be voices for social justice, support young people, and follow our inner guidance. We can reject the values of raunch in favor of love, connection, community, and intimacy.

ACKNOWLEDGMENTS

It is a pleasure to appreciate and acknowledge all of the many individuals who contributed to this book! I am grateful to those who agreed to talk about raunch culture, especially the students who offered their impressions in and out of the classroom. As challenging as it can be at times to be a feminist professor in a sexist culture, my students give me hope and joy. I thank two decades of curious, engaged, generous students who fearlessly shared insights about contemporary culture, and sometimes their personal experiences with the issues explored here.

Many colleagues, friends, and family supported the creation of this book. I appreciate Kristen Barber, Colin V. Barton, Kathleen M. Blee, Lisa Hinkle Bond, Susan Bordo, Ric Caric, Charles H. Combs, Karen Cornett Ashley Currier, Scott Davison Elicia Elfers, Breanne Fahs, Cynthia Faulkner, Janet Gallaway, Abby Geurin, Katie Goldey, Caitlin Haggard, Shelbi Hall, Constance L. Hardesty, Sylvia Henneberg, Michael C. Henson, Lisa Huebner, Emily Jo Jackson, Juniper James Jacques, Patricia K. Jennings, Jeffrey A. Jones, Ran Keren, Albina Laskovtsov, Amber Elane Lawson, Hannah Mabry, Kristen Mark, Patricia Yancey Martin, Marie Miller, Dianna Murphy, Shondrah Tarrezz Nash, Vanessa Ramirez, Sharon Scales Rostosky, William Rothwell, Alexandra Teitz, Leah Teuwen, Dave Weiland, and anonymous reviewers with NYU Press. I would also like to acknowledge journalist Ariel Levy's work in her cutting-edge book *Female Chauvinist Pigs: Women and the Rise of Raunch Culture* for vividly making visible the phenomenon of raunch culture for me. I am following a path she first carved.

This work also greatly benefitted from institutional support. Many thanks to the Office of Research and Sponsored Programs, the Caudill College of Arts, Humanities, and Social Sciences, and the Department of

Sociology, Social Work, and Criminology at Morehead State University for providing research and travel funds, and release time, to complete this project.

I continue to feel enormously lucky to publish with NYU Press, and grateful to the hard-working, excellent, meticulous staff. Special thanks to Sonia Tsuruoka, Martin Coleman, Dan Geist, Mary Beth Jarrad, Betsy Steve, Sarah Bode, Sydney Garcia, and Ilene Kalish. I've enjoyed a decade-plus long relationship with Ilene, editor extraordinaire, and deeply appreciate the distinctive combination of kindness, thoughtfulness, rigor, and framing that she brings to a manuscript. On my fourth book with Ilene, I am enormously conscious of, and grateful for, the intelligence and care she puts into my books, and the hundreds of books she has manifested into the world.

Finally, I recognize my wife, Anna Blanton, my anchor and heart, who continues to support my demanding, provocative, and controversial projects even when they drive her crazy. Much love to you, Anna!

NOTES

INTRODUCTION

1 Journalist Pamela Paul coined the term "pornified" in 2005.
2 Landsbaum 2016.
3 In February 2016, Puzder withdrew his name from consideration for labor secretary not because of an outcry over the institutionalized sexism he promoted in Hardee's and Carl's Jr. advertisements, but because of controversy over allegations of abuse from his ex-wife and his hiring of an undocumented immigrant to work as his housekeeper.
4 Berman 2018.
5 The story even includes sinister Russian agents intent on destroying American democracy with futuristic computer technology.
6 Consider the original Amazon show *Fleabag* (2016): during the first episode an anonymous male hookup penetrates a woman anally while she is asleep and she treats it as an *accomplishment*.
7 Attwood 2006; Barton 2017; Dines 2010; Douglas 2010; Evans, Riley, and Shanker 2010; Friedman 2017; Gill 2007, 2008, 2012; Levy 2005; Oppliger 2008; Palmer 2012; Tanenbaum 2015; Walter 2015; Wesley 2012.
8 McNair 2009; Paul 2005.
9 Holland and Atwood 2009; Pollet and Hurwitz 2003.
10 Barton 2017.
11 Douglas 2010; McNair 2002.
12 Wolf 1991.
13 Bordo 1993; Jhally 2010.
14 For a detailed description and analysis of Western media texts through the 1990s and 2000s, see Douglas 2010.
15 Douglas 2010, 182.
16 Sheets 2019.
17 Connell and Messerschmidt 2005.
18 Perry and Sanchez 1998.
19 Kimmel 2017.
20 Lerner 1986.
21 Wade 2017.
22 Wade 2017.

23 These include the women's, antiwar, civil rights, gay rights, and anti-apartheid movements and the sexual revolution.

24 APA 2007.

25 Douglas 2010; Gill 2007.

26 Douglas 2010; Levy 2005.

27 Friedman 2017.

28 Here I further develop a concept I originated in my work on the lives of Bible Belt gays. In *Pray the Gay Away* (2012), I use the "condition of inarticulation" to explore the effects of closeting. Among the many issues that occur within the "toxic closet" is a silencing of daily communicative exchanges in which closeted gay persons cannot discuss their partners and their joint activities like heterosexuals routinely do.

29 Philosopher Miranda Fricker (2007) explores this in her work on the hermeneutical injustice, which she describes as occurring when people lack the conceptual resources to understand their experiences, especially in the case of minority group members interpreting and naming inequity.

30 "Talking back" is the act of speaking as an equal to an authority. A speech act that liberates oppressed people, it was developed theoretically by bell hooks.

31 *Stripped: Inside the Lives of Exotic Dancers* (2006) and *Stripped: More Stories from Exotic Dancers* (2017).

32 SodaHead.com, "Jennifer Aniston Is a Stripper in a New Movie Role, Who Is Your Favorite Good Girl Gone Bad?," May 24, 2013, Fox News, www.foxnews.com.

33 Fahs 2014.

34 Dines 2010; Dworkin 1974.

35 Chapkis 1997.

36 Barton 2002, 2015.

37 Barton 2006, 2017.

38 Duggan and Hunter 2006; Fahs 2014.

39 Chapkis 1997; Vance 1984.

40 Barton 2002, 2006, 2015, 2017.

41 Chancer 1998; Fahs 2014.

42 Singer 2017.

43 Queen and Comella 2008.

44 Engeln 2017.

45 Eltahawy 2015.

46 Barton 2017.

47 Armstrong, England, and Fogarty 2018; Collins 2004; McLaurin 1991.

48 Wade 2017, 95.

49 Ingraham and Saunders 2016.

50 Dean 2014; Doane and Bonilla-Silva 2003; Ward 2020.

51 Herzog 2008.

52 All of the names of my students and interviewees in this book are pseudonyms.

53 Levey 2018; Phillips 2015; Poland 2016.

54 Hlavka 2014.

55 Bridges et al. 2010.

56 England, Shafer, and Fogarty 2007; Wade 2017.

57 Most of the interview subjects were unfamiliar with the term "raunch culture," but once I explained it to them as the hypersexualization of culture using sample images and we discussed it, they well perceived it.

58 The book draws on interviews with 67 people ranging in age from 18 to 76 that took place between July 2016 and April 2019. Fifty-three of the interview subjects are millennials or Gen Z, which means they were 18–35 when they were interviewed. Subjects include 47 women and 20 men. Six identify as Latinx, three as black, and the remainder are white. Four participants are pansexual, nine bisexual, six gay/lesbian, and the rest are heterosexual. In-depth audiotaped interviews, content analysis of media texts, 25 years of classroom conversations with students exploring representations of gender in the media, and years of researching the sex industry equally inform the description and analysis of raunch culture advanced herein. The participants are a convenience sample, composed of former students, friends of students, neighbors, and acquaintances. Each interview lasted from 30 to 90 minutes and took place at a location convenient to the participant, usually my house, their home, or a quiet public place. I used a semistructured interview guide, asking people to define raunch culture, share what they think of it, offer examples of raunch in their daily experience, and explore the impact of the hypersexualization in their lives and the lives of those they know. I also asked participants to reflect upon generational differences in how people experience raunch culture and, finally, share their thoughts on how we might transform it. I received IRB approval to conduct this study and obtained informed consent from each participant. Each interview was recorded and transcribed in full. I coded the transcripts for themes related to the interview questions and noted patterns that emerged in participants' comments.

   At the suggestion of reviewers, I expanded the age range of participants from millennials and Generation Z to include older generations. The ideas and insights of older people illustrate how raunch culture is not just about youth, but about the culture. I did find that the older the interview participant, generally the less aware and engaged they were with raunch culture, especially those in their 70s. If a participant was unfamiliar with the term "raunch culture," I explained it at the beginning of the interview. I did this in approximately 90% of the interviews. Copies of advertisements and shots from music videos easily illuminated it.

CHAPTER 1. WHAT MEN SEE, WHAT MEN WANT

1 All the images shown in the previous chapter illustrate the male gaze alongside raunch culture. They differ in that raunch culture encompasses most of Western

social life—including how people talk, dress, and behave—while the male gaze theory limits itself to how people see and read visual media.

2 The male gaze predates raunch culture, and is visible in Renaissance art, and print and film media throughout the 20th century. John Berger explored the representations of women in Renaissance paintings in a televised BBC series, later developing his analysis into the book *Ways of Seeing* (1973). Berger found that men act while women merely appear in Renaissance art. Sociologist Erving Goffman explored how femininity and masculinity are portrayed in Western media in his book *Gender Advertisements* (1976). Goffman observed that men in advertisements were portrayed as confident, comfortable, and active. In contrast, advertisers posed women as soft, languid, vulnerable, dreamy, and touching their own bodies. Viewers can see most of these socially constructed gender codes in contemporary advertising. Documentarian Sut Jhally applies Goffman's analysis to 21st-century media in his film *The Codes of Gender* (2009). Beginning in a systematic, sustained way in the mid-1990s, advertisers have layered hypersexualization into ads.

3 Mulvey 1975.

4 I found these at "Feature Film, Action, Damsel-in-Distress (Sorted by Popularity Ascending)," IMDB, www.imdb.com/search/title?genres=action&keywords=damsel-in-distress&sort=moviemeter&title_type=feature&fbclid=IwAR0WJ997JJofN3gJsTvP8PZDp_Vd4AP-ada-Z1KGJ8wpEpjC4gGe4gJYDg8. I reference here the top few from a list of 1,416 such films.

5 Geena Davis Institute of Gender in Media, *The Reel Truth: Women Aren't Seen or Heard: An Automated Analysis of Gender Representation in Popular Films*, 2015, https://seejane.org.

6 Kilday 2019: "One key to boosting the number of women on a production was having a female director. Among the top 500 films, [in] those with at least one female director, women made up 71 percent of writers, 47 percent of editors, 19 percent of cinematographers and 24 percent of composers."

7 North 2018; Bloodworth-Thomason 2018. In fall 2018, television writer Linda Bloodworth-Thomason exposed the sustained and systematic silencing of women's voices that had taken place at CBS under Moonves. She detailed how Les Moonves sabotaged every show she proposed starting in 1995, thus potentially cheating viewers out of decades of woman-centered programming.

8 Smith, Choueiti, and Pieper 2016. Within each racial group (white, Latinx, black, Asian, and other), the authors found a two-to-one representation of male to female characters.

9 Smith, Choueiti, and Pieper 2016.

10 Erigha 2019, 5–6.

11 Ford 2019.

12 For analysis, see the documentaries *Latinos beyond Reel* (Picker and Sun 2012), *Mickey Mouse Monopoly* (Sun and Picker 2001), *Generation M* (Thomas 2008), and *Miss Representation* (Newsom 2011).

13 Hall 2000, 277. This is a form of what W. E. B. DuBois (1903) theorized as "double consciousness," in which black people see themselves through their own eyes as well as the gaze of white culture.

14 Bailey 2010.

15 hooks 1994; Hunter and Soto 2009.

16 hooks 1989.

17 After conducting content analysis on the lyrics of popular rap songs, sociologists Hunter and Soto (2009) found that sex work is also commonly mentioned. They found that "nearly a third of songs contained overt references to stripping, prostitution, or pornography" (176).

18 Hurt 2006.

19 "Chickenhead" is a derogatory term that mocks the motion of giving a man oral sex.

20 Resnikoff 2014.

21 Hurt 2006.

22 Manne 2017.

23 Media scholar George Gerbner (1967) originated and developed cultivation theory. As Potter (2014) explains, "Gerbner was not interested in the influence of particular message elements; instead he was interested in widespread meanings across the entire media landscape. He was not concerned with how people selected messages for exposure, nor how they processed the information in those messages, nor what effects particular messages exerted on people during exposures or immediately after; instead, he was exclusively concerned with the influence that a much broader scope of messages gradually exerted on the public as people were exposed to media messages in their everyday lives" (1016).

24 Jhally 2008.

25 Anderson 2018.

26 Valdes 1996, 162.

27 Ariel Levy (2005) explores a dimension of androsexism in her description of "female chauvinist pigs."

28 I previously developed the concept of "bro-privilege"—then referring to it as "andro-privilege"—with my co-author Hannah Mabry in our 2018 article "Andro-privilege, Raunch Culture, and Stripping." It builds on the work of feminist theorists like Patricia Hill Collins, Abby Ferber, Allan Johnson, and Peggy McIntosh.

29 Author Gillian Flynn vividly describes the "cool girl" in her novel *Gone Girl* (2014): "Men always say that as *the* defining compliment, don't they? *She's a cool girl*. Being the Cool Girl means I am a hot, brilliant, funny woman who adores football, poker, dirty jokes, and burping, who plays video games, drinks cheap beer, loves threesomes and anal sex, and jams hot dogs and hamburgers into her mouth like she's hosting the world's biggest culinary gang bang while somehow

maintaining a size 2, because Cool Girls are above all hot. Hot and understanding. Cool Girls never get angry; they only smile in a chagrined, loving manner and let their men do whatever they want. *Go ahead, shit on me, I don't mind, I'm the Cool Girl"* (222).

30 McRobbie 2008.

31 To illustrate, during the 2014 Gamergate controversy, several women experienced vicious and sustained misogynist attacks, including online rape and death threats, after critiquing the sexism they encountered in video game culture (Suellentrop 2014).

32 Hochschild and Machung 2012. Sociologist Arlie Hochschild describes this as a "stalled revolution."

33 While new grooming habits of men suggest some cultural feminization, sociologist Kristen Barber (2016) situates these habits as a class-based gender body project that allows middle- and upper-class men to distinguish themselves from poor and working-class ones. Further, those selling style services to men do so specifically using language coded masculine to uphold their manliness.

34 Manne 2017.

35 Pharr 1996.

36 See Hamilton (2007) for an analysis of heterosexual college women's performance of same-sex eroticism for male audiences.

37 Barton 2017; Barton and Mabry 2018.

38 Hamilton 2007.

39 Klaassen 2010.

40 Nestle 1992.

41 This is not to say that all lesbians resist practicing sexism. Some lesbians assume bro-privilege because identifying with power is attractive and, again, a respite from oppression. My point here is that butch gender expression does not equal bro-privilege, although butch women may sometimes adopt it.

42 First theorized by Deniz Kandiyoti in 1988, a patriarchal bargain offers individual women personal advantages for accommodating patriarchal norms that disadvantage women as a group.

CHAPTER 2. HOW INTERNET PORNOGRAPHY RUINS SEX

1 Brown and L'Engle 2009; Sabina, Wolak, and Finkelhor 2008.

2 Dines 2010.

3 Sun et al. 2016.

4 Barton 2017; McNair 2009.

5 One of the earliest erotic film dates to 1896: *Le coucher de la mariée.*

6 Buzzell 2005.

7 Attwood 2009; Dines 2010; McCullough 2015; Paasonen 2011.

8 Paasonen 2011.

9   Andrea Dworkin's *Woman Hating* (1974) details the cultural subordination of women in fairy tales, pornography, and cultural practices like Chinese foot binding.

10 Sun et al. 2016; Jensen 2007; Manne 2017.

11 Internet pornography well illustrates sociologist Patricia Hill Collins's (2000) theoretical concept of "controlling images," that is, stereotyped representations of a subordinate group developed and disseminated by members of a dominant group to justify their oppression.

12 Bridges et al. 2010.

13 Phone traffic to Pornhub increased 5% from 2016 to 2017, totaling 67% of all traffic to the site.

14 Barton 2017.

15 A national survey of sexual health conducted by researchers at Indiana University found that 81–84% of men aged 18–39 had masturbated alone in the past year. Indiana University Bloomington School of Public Health, *National Survey of Sexual Health and Behavior*, 2019, www.nationalsexstudy.indiana.edu.

16 "Pornhub's 2016 Year in Review," January 4, 2017, www.pornhub.com.

17 For a history of internet pornography, see McCullough 2015.

18 Dines 2006; Jensen 2007; Sun and Picker 2008.

19 A nationally representative sex survey found that 35% of men found anal sex very or somewhat appealing, compared to 14% of women (Herbenick et al. 2017).

20 Dines 2010.

21 Barton 2012. This is also a good illustration of the kind of same sex behavior heterosexual men have with one another in the service of heterosexuality that Jane Ward explores in her book *Not Gay* (2015).

22 "Bukkake" is a Japanese word. It describes the practice of several men ejaculating onto a woman. For example, a woman is tied up and gagged with men circling her masturbating together and ejaculating on her face and body.

23 Sun et al. 2016.

24 We began class an excited, happy, smiling group and then, after viewing the compilation, which ran a long 25 minutes, we sat there silent, shocked, and disturbed. Not only did we talk about the compilation after we watched it, I also asked them to write about it in their final exam. A content analysis of their responses found that the terms they most commonly used were: "disgust/disgusted/disgusting," "bad," "worse/worst," "cry," "young/younger," "rape/rapes," "degrade/degraded/degrading/degradation," "it pissed me off/ it made me angry," "enjoy/enjoying/enjoyed" (not that they enjoyed it, but questioned how others could).

25 May 2015; Snow 2017. News sources began covering the rise in fauxcest porn in 2015. Gareth May writes, "A report by leading multimedia-adult-content providers GameLink.com revealed a 178 percent average increase in the consumption of

'family role-play porn' between October 2014 and January 2015. The stats show Utah had the highest increase with 765 percent; Michigan (698 percent), New York (669 percent), Alaska (524 percent), and Arkansas (452 percent) made up the five states where incest porn was growing in popularity the fastest. According to GameLink, the ten most popular family role play porn titles are: *Father's Forbidden Fantasies, Friends and Family 4, Mother's Indiscretions #3, Keep It in the Family, Brothers & Sisters 2, Mommy and Me #9, Lesbian Family Affairs, Father's Day, Digital Sin, Sibling Sex Stories,* and, most sinister of all for some reason, *Our Father.*"

26 As creepy and disturbing as it was that the students in 2019 found and documented so much incest-centered porn, there was one hopeful note: the porn they shared was less violent than that collected by the 2013 group. Perhaps the early to mid-2010s was the apex of violent pornography. Only time will tell.

27 Paul 2005. A 2016 survey of 487 college men exploring how pornography use affected their sexual encounters found that the more pornography a man watched, the more likely he was to use it during sex, and ask for his partner to perform particular pornographic sex acts (Sun et al. 2016).

28 Diefendorf 2015.

29 Some sex researchers argue that "pornography addiction" does not meet the classificatory standards of addiction (Ley, Prause, and Finn 2014). Narrowly defined, addiction is associated with changes in neural circuits in the brain related to substance use. Ley, Prause, and Finn write, "While there seems to be a consensus that addiction is a useful construct to describe opiate dependence, the usefulness of 'addiction' to describe the excessive use of any drug, compulsive gambling, and excessive video game playing has raised many concerns" (96). Despite this analysis, in June 2018 the World Health Organization added "compulsive sexual behavior disorder" to its list of mental health disorders. Likely unfamiliar with the clinical debate over whether problematic and disruptive sexual behavior constitutes addiction, several participants, like Jordan, used the language of addiction in relation to pornography.

30 Armstrong, England, and Fogarty 2012.

31 Bogle 2008; Currier 2013; Freitas 2013; Lovejoy 2012.

32 Freitas 2013; Ronen 2010.

33 Galliano 1993.

34 Moller 2017, 932. A 2017 study of 298 rape survivors found that 70% of the women had experienced tonic immobility during an assault and 48% reported extreme tonic immobility. In other words, tonic immobility is a common response to sexual assault, although some still judge whether a rape occurred based on the woman's degree of resistance.

35 Park et al. 2016; Paul 2005; Wilson 2012.

36 Kohut, Fisher, and Campbell 2017.

37 Stewart and Szymanski 2012, 257.

38 Olmstead et al. 2013; Rothman et al. 2015.

39 May 2015.

40 Dines 2010; Wilson 2012.

41 Fields 2016.

42 Pinker 2011.

43 Dines 2010; Media Foundation Education, "Media Violence: Facts & Statistics," 2005, www.mediaed.org.

44 Twenge, Sherman, and Wells 2017.

CHAPTER 3. "BE THE MAN THAT TREATS HER LIKE A LADY, BUT STILL GRABS HER ASS"

1 Andrew Hutchinson, "Top Social Network Demographics 2017," March 21, 2017, Social Media Today, www.socialmediatoday.com.

2 "Tinder Information, Statistics, Facts, and History," Dating Sites Reviews, www.datingsitesreviews.com.

3 "Snapchat by the Numbers, Demographics, and Fun Facts," September 5, 2019, Omnicore, www.omnicoreagency.com.

4 Jennifer Leslie, "55 Social Media Marketing Stats and Facts for 2018," February 1, 2018, Keap, https://learn.infusionsoft.com.

5 Salim 2019.

6 Aiken 2016; Alter 2017; Bauerlein 2011; Freitas 2017; Rushkoff 2013; Turkle 2015.

7 Turkle 2015, 73.

8 Aiken 2016; Alter 2017.

9 "How Much Time Do People Spend on Their Mobile Phones in 2017," May 9, 2017, Hackernoon, https://hackernoon.com.

10 Lyubomirsky 2013.

11 Goffman 1959.

12 Freitas 2017.

13 Belic 2011.

14 Tromholt 2016; Turel, Cavagnaro, and Meshi 2018.

15 Deepa Lakshmin, "How Does Snapchat Choose Your Best Friends List? We Investigated," February 25, 2015, MTV, www.mtv.com.

16 In 2015, recognizing that the top three friends ranking was an issue for users, Snapchat changed this feature from a ranking that all one's friends could see to private friend emojis that tell a user who one is snapping most often, as well as the ratio between how often one snaps another individual and how often that person snaps one in turn.

17 Friedman 2016.

18 Marwick and Boyd 2011.

19 I argue that it is often better not to know these factoids about others, especially coldly learning them on a screen absent a personal connection and the ability to

talk through the news. I say this because of the emotional repercussions I both experienced and documented related to political events in 2004 (Barton 2012). At that time Kentucky, as well as many other states, had an anti-gay marriage initiative on the ballot and the region was swimming in signage advocating "Yes on Amendment 1," a referendum on a constitutional amendment to ban same-sex marriage in the state. I was living in a small town with my partner of six years and recall how upset I felt seeing "Vote Yes for Amendment 1" on car bumper stickers. When our next-door neighbor set up a pro–Amendment 1 yard sign, it became an ordeal just to pull into my own driveway. The environment of a platform like Facebook means users may come across similarly upsetting and polarizing communications 24/7.

20 Engeln 2017.

21 Freitas 2017; O'Reilly et al. 2018; Primack et al. 2017; Vogel et al. 2014; Woods and Scott 2016; Yoon et al. 2019.

22 Fredrickson and Roberts 1997.

23 Sales 2016.

24 Alter 2017; Sales 2016.

25 Nonetheless, most of those who comment on women's bodies are still men. Brian estimated that "for every one comment from a girl, there's probably 10 or 15 comments from guys."

26 Hochschild and Machung 2012.

27 Myers 2017.

28 Daniels 2016, 8.

29 Potter 2004, 269–270.

30 Dines 2010, 105.

CHAPTER 4. DICK PICS

1 Chatroulette has since faded in popularity, although a much smaller number of people—mostly men—still use the site, primarily for masturbation. Azar, an app launched by the Korean company Hyperconnect, is an updated version of Chatroulette that also pairs people in random video chats through their mobile devices. Users of Azar also have to fend off random dick pics.

2 Suler 2004. The author distinguishes between benign and toxic disinhibition. Benign disinhibition involves disclosing very personal information about oneself—secrets and fears for example. Threats, hate speech, and insults, along with unwanted and unsolicited sexual communications, are examples of toxic disinhibition.

3 Suler 2004, 321.

4 Friedman 2017; Jane 2015; Noble 2018; Poland 2016.

5 DeKeseredy and Schwartz 2016; Freitas 2017.

6 Egan 2013.

7 Best and Bogle 2014.

8 Madigan et al. 2018.

9 Englander 2015.

10 Burén and Lunde 2018.

11 Kreager and Staff 2009; Ringrose et al. 2013; Salter 2016.

12 Best and Bogle 2014; Egan 2013.

13 Zickl 2017.

14 "Singles & Sex," 2017, Singles in America, www.singlesinamerica.com.

15 Former US representative Anthony Weiner from New York resigned in 2011 after he sent a dick pic to a woman on Twitter.

16 Hayes and Dragiewicz 2018.

17 Hayes and Dragiewicz (2018) argue that dick pics are a contemporary version of flashing.

18 Lebowitz 2016.

19 Kimmel 2013.

20 "Exhibitionism," 2019, Psychology Today, www.psychologytoday.com; Freund and Blanchard 1986.

21 Pharr 1996. The Quakers were the first to use the phrase "speak truth to power."

22 Fredrickson and Roberts 1997; Phillips 2000, 125.

23 Tolman 2002.

24 Mandau 2019, 72.

25 Segran and Truong 2016.

26 Ansari 2015.

27 Bendixen 2014.

28 Kohn 2018.

29 Abbey 1982.

30 Segran and Truong 2016.

31 Dickson 2017.

CHAPTER 5. TRUMP'S RAUNCH CULTURE ADMINISTRATION

1 Sociologist Arlie Hochschild developed the concept of the stalled revolution in her book with Anne Machung, The Second Shift (2012). The stalled revolution describes the phenomenon in which women adopt some of the values and responsibilities coded "masculine" like working outside the home, but men do not likewise embrace behaviors coded feminine.

2 Including, of course, Hillary Clinton's book What Happened (2017). Much has been written on the faux email scandal James Comey insisted on investigating (Bordo 2017), the backlash to decades of neoliberal policies, the rise of nationalism (Manza and Crowley 2018), the influence of Fox News and alt-right media (Daniels 2018), anti-immigrant rhetoric (Romero 2018), gerrymandering, Hillary hatred (Bordo 2017), GOP witch hunts, disgruntled Sanders voters (Bordo 2017), frustrated rural voters (Hochschild 2016), racism, misogyny, sexism, American manhood (Katz 2016), and, most troublingly, Russian hacks of the election and

collusion with the Trump campaign (Clinton 2017; Harding 2017; Jamieson 2018; Snyder 2018).

3 Jane 2015, 65.

4 Jane 2015. Jane observes that even as we see more and more e-bile in digital culture, scholarly work on it has decreased. This is partly due to the glacial pace of academic publishing. Also, like much of the scholarship on internet pornography, research on digital communications favors celebratory and optimistic readings of hostile content, frames those who have an issue with it as overly sensitive and humorless, and in general ignores the gender inequality on display.

5 Jane 2015, 67.

6 Lumsden and Morgan 2012.

7 Jamieson 2018; Parlapiano and Lee 2018.

8 "Trolling Tay: Microsoft's New AI Chatbot Censored after Racist & Sexist Tweets," March 24, 2016, RT, www.rt.com.

9 Meyer 2016. Peter Lee (2016), vice president of Microsoft Research, issued an apology on the Official Microsoft Blog, explaining, "We stress-tested Tay under a variety of conditions, specifically to make interacting with Tay a positive experience. Once we got comfortable with how Tay was interacting with users, we wanted to invite a broader group of people to engage with her. It's through increased interaction where we expected to learn more and for the AI to get better and better."

10 Archer 2018.

11 Jane 2015.

12 West 2015.

13 Lewis 2018.

14 Connell 1995.

15 Jensen 2007.

16 Allen and Swan 2017.

17 Fuller 2016.

18 "Donald Trump—The Howard Stern Interviews 1993–2015," Factbase, https://factba.se.

19 Relman 2019.

20 Withnall 2016.

21 Cohen 2017.

22 Boboltz 2019.

23 "MAGA (Make America Great Again) Bikinis Multiply!," July 19, 2017, Tea Party, www.teaparty.org.

24 This catchy phrase was coined to encourage Christian women to stay covered so as not to arouse the boys and men who may see them. For a discussion of the phrase and its origins, see Erin, "Modest Is Hottest?: What Is Your Take on Modesty?," May 9, 2016, Odyssey, www.theodysseyonline.com.

25 "Voters More Focused on Control of Congress—and the President—than in Past Midterms," June 20, 2018, Pew Research Center, www.people-press.org.

26 See Fea 2018; Kuruvilla 2018; Pollitt 2018; Whitehead, Perry, and Baker 2018; Wilson-Hartgrove 2018.

27 Jessica Martinez and Gregory A. Smith, "How the Faithful Voted: A Preliminary 2016 Analysis," November 9, 2016, Pew Research Center, www. pewresearch.org.

28 Ehrenreich 2018.

29 Fitzgerald 2017; Worthen 2017.

30 Whitehead, Perry, and Baker 2018.

31 From the official media outlet of the Christian Nationalist Alliance. "FAQ," Christian Nationalism, www.christiannationalism.com.

32 Herzog 2008, 31.

33 Burke 2016.

34 Fahrenthold 2016.

35 Mindock 2018.

36 Bauman 2018.

37 Modi 2018.

38 "The Year in Hate: Trump Buoyed White Supremacists in 2017, Sparking Backlash among Black Nationalist Groups," February 21, 2018, Southern Poverty Law Center, www.splcenter.org.

39 Chaudhry and Tucker 2017.

40 Eligon 2018.

41 Horowitz, Brown, and Cox 2019.

42 Conti 2016. A national poll conducted by Reuters/Ipsos and researchers at the University of Virginia Center for Politics after the neo-Nazi rally in Charlottesville in August 2017 substantiates Mike's estimation. While only 8% of respondents supported "white nationalism," 31% agreed or strongly agreed that the US needs to "protect and preserve its White European heritage." See UVA Center for Politics, "New Poll: Some Americans Express Troubling Racial Attitudes Even as Majority Oppose White Supremacists," September 14, 2017, www.centerforpolitics.org.

43 In the words of Brazilian philosopher Paulo Freire (2018), "the oppressors are afraid of losing the 'freedom' to oppress" (46). Also see Solnit 2018.

44 Henley and Pincus 1978; Herek 1987; Whitley 1999; Whitley and Egisdottir 2000. There is also much research finding a relationship between prejudice, right-wing authoritarianism and dimensions of religiosity. See, e.g., Altemeyer and Hunsberger 1992; Fisher et al. 1994; Kirkpatrick 1993; Laythe, Finkel, and Kirkpatrick 2001; Whitley and Lee 2000; Whitley 1999; Whitley and Egisdottir 2000.

45 Glick and Fiske 1996.

46 Glick and Fiske 1996, 109.

47 See Susan Bordo's fascinating and insightful book *The Destruction of Hillary Clinton* (2017). You can also watch a grueling six minutes of sexist attacks on Hillary Clinton compiled by mediamatters4america, "The Media's Years of Sexist Attacks on Hillary Clinton," at www.youtube.com/watch?v=i_7GrRw6S64.

48 A Trump supporter sent bombs to the Clintons, Obamas, Eric Holder, CNN, George Soros, and others in October 2018, and crowds are still chanting "lock her up" about Hillary Clinton. Trump has also encouraged supporters to "lock up" democrats Dianne Feinstein and Nancy Pelosi.

49 Starhawk 1993, 44.

50 Starhawk 1993, 44.

CHAPTER 6. TRANSFORMING RAUNCH CULTURE

1 The Sapir-Whorf hypothesis argues that language influences how we perceive and think about the world (O'Neill 2015).

2 Veiga Mateos and Saxon 2017.

3 Kamenetz 2017.

4 Manne 2017.

5 Goled 2019.

6 Trans-exclusionary radical feminists see gender as the root oppression and argue that no one would be interested in changing their sex from female to male or male to female were a wide range of gender expression common and accepted in daily life. This group of feminists is more interested in changing gender norms than supporting trans rights.

7 Studies find that abstinence-only sex education has a number of harmful consequences in young people's lives, including higher rates of pregnancy and STIs (Santelli et al. 2017).

8 There are good sources of educational pornography one can find online, like the Sinclair Institute series. However, again, this educational series will not come up on a porn search and must be searched for specifically.

9 I feel so strongly about this, I devote a class period every semester in my gender classes to an open, anonymous Q&A on sex education. The students write down any question they have about sexuality—nothing is off-limits—without their names on it. Everyone has to submit a paper even if it is blank so that no one's question can be identified. I then read their questions aloud and answer them. The rules are that I don't have to answer something if it makes me uncomfortable, though that has not happened yet, and that if I don't know the answer, I say so, and we try to figure it out together.

10 Lukianoff and Haidt 2018.

11 Sanson, Strange, and Garry 2019.

12 Morgan 1970, xx.

13 Gose and Skocpol 2018.

14 De Beauvoir 1952; Hurtado 1989; Moraga and Anzaldúa 2015.

15 Jones 2020.

16 See "Pornhub Insights: Coronavirus Update—April 14," April 14, 2020, Pornhub, www.pornhub.com.

REFERENCES

Abbey, Antonia. 1982. "Sex Differences in Attributions for Friendly Behavior: Do Males Misperceive Females' Friendliness?" *Journal of Personality and Social Psychology* 42(5): 830–838.

Aiken, Mary. 2017. *The Cyber Effect: An Expert in Cyberpsychology Explains How Technology Is Shaping Our Children, Our Behavior, and Our Values and What We Can Do about It.* New York: Spiegel & Grau.

Allen, Mike, and Jonathan Swan. February 2, 2017. "Trump 101: The Producer of His Own Epic Film." *Axios.* www.axios.com.

Altemeyer, Bob, and Bruce Hunsberger. 1992. "Authoritarianism, Religious Fundamentalism, Quest, and Prejudice." *International Journal for the Psychology of Religion* 2 (2): 113–133.

Alter, Adam. 2017. *Irresistible: The Rise of Addictive Technology and the Business of Keeping Us Hooked.* New York: Penguin Books.

Anderson, Mae. December 5, 2018. "Report Details New Allegations of CBS Exec Les Moonves' Sexual Misconduct." *Chicago Tribune.* www.chicagotribune.com.

Ansari, Aziz, with Eric Klinenberg. 2015. *Modern Romance.* New York: Penguin Books.

APA (American Psychological Association Task Force). 2007. *Report of the APA Task Force on the Sexualization of Girls.* Washington, DC. www.apa.org.

Archer, Nandini. August 14, 2018. "'Feminism Is Cancer': The Angry Backlash against Our Reporting on the Men's Rights Movement." *50.50.* www.opendemocracy.net.

Armstrong, Elizabeth A., Paula England, and Alison C. K. Fogarty. 2012. "Accounting for Women's Orgasm and Sexual Enjoyment in College Hookups and Relationships." *American Sociological Review* 77(3): 435–462.

Attwood, Feona. 2006. "Sexed Up: Theorizing the Sexualization of Culture." *Sexualities* 9(1): 77–94.

———. 2009. *Porn.com: Making Sense of Online Pornography.* New York: Peter Lang.

Bailey, Moya. March 14, 2010. "They Aren't Talking about Me . . . ." *Crunk Feminist Collective.* www.crunkfeministcollective.com.

Barber, Kristen. 2016. *Styling Masculinity: Gender, Class, and Inequality in the Men's Grooming Industry.* New Brunswick, NJ: Rutgers University Press.

Barton, Bernadette. 2002. "Dancing on the Möbius Strip: Challenging the Sex War Paradigm." *Gender and Society* 16(5): 585–602.

———. 2006. *Stripped: Inside the Lives of Exotic Dancers.* New York: NYU Press.

———. 2012. *Pray the Gay Away: The Extraordinary Lives of Bible Belt Gays*. New York: NYU Press.

———. 2015. "Freedom from Sexism vs. Sexual Freedom: A Short History of the Feminist Sex Wars." In *Provocations: A Transnational, Historical Reader in Feminist Thought*, edited by Susan Bordo, M. Christine Alcade, and Ellen Rosenman. Berkeley: University of California Press, pp. 430–436.

———. 2017. *Stripped: More Stories from Exotic Dancers*. New York: NYU Press.

Barton, Bernadette, and Hannah Mabry. 2018. "Andro-privilege, Raunch Culture, and Stripping." *Sexualities* 21(4): 605–620.

Bauerlein, Mark, ed. 2011. *The Digital Divide: Arguments for and against Facebook, Google, Texting, and the Age of Social Networking*. New York: Penguin Books.

Bauman, Dan. February 16, 2018. "After 2016 Election, Campus Hate Crimes Seemed to Jump. Here's What the Data Tell Us." *Chronicle of Higher Education*. www.chronicle.com.

Belic, Roko, dir. 2011. *Happy*. Passion River Films.

Bendixen, Mons. 2014. "Evidence of Systematic Bias in Sexual Over- and Underperception of Naturally Occurring Events: A Direct Replication of in a More Gender-Equal Culture." *Evolutionary Psychology* 12(5). DOI: 147470491401200510.

Berger, John. 1973. *Ways of Seeing*. London: BBC/Penguin Books.

Berman, Robby. May 4, 2018. "Where in the World Sugar Daddies Thrive, Why, and What's Being Done about It." *Big Think*. http://bigthink.com.

Best, Joel, and Kathleen A. Bogle. 2014. *Kids Gone Wild: From Rainbow Parties to Sexting, Understanding the Hype over Teen Sex*. New York: NYU Press.

Bloodworth-Thomason, Linda. September 12, 2018. "'Designing Women' Creator Goes Public with Les Moonves War: Not All Harassment Is Sexual." *Hollywood Reporter*. www.hollywoodreporter.com.

Boboltz, Sara. July 11, 2019. "A Timeline of Sex Offender Jeffrey Epstein's Convictions and New Allegations." *HuffPost*. www.huffpost.com.

Bogle, Kathleen A. 2008. *Hooking Up: Sex, Dating, and Relationships on Campus*. New York: NYU Press.

Bordo, Susan. 1993. *Unbearable Weight: Feminism, Western Culture, and the Body*. Berkeley: University of California Press.

———. 2017. *The Destruction of Hillary Clinton*. Melbourne: Text Publishing.

Bridges, Ana, Robert Wosnitzer, Erica Scharrer, Chyng Sun, and Rachael Liberman. 2010. "Aggression and Sexual Behavior in Best-Selling Pornography Videos: A Content Analysis Update." *Violence against Women* 16(10): 1065–1085.

Brown, Jane D., and Kelly L. L'Engle. 2009. "X-rated: Sexual Attitudes and Behaviors Associated with US Early Adolescents' Exposure to Sexually Explicit Media." *Communication Research* 36(1): 129–151.

Burén, Jonas, and Carolina Lunde. 2018. "Sexting among Adolescents: A Nuanced and Gendered Online Challenge for Young People." *Computers in Human Behavior* 85: 210–217.

Burke, Kelsy. 2016. *Christians under Covers: Evangelicals and Sexual Pleasure on the Internet*. Berkeley: University of California Press.

Buzzell, Timothy. 2005. "Demographic Characteristics of Persons Using Pornography in Three Technological Contexts." *Sexuality & Culture* 9(1): 28–48.

Chancer, Lynn. 1998. *Reconcilable Differences: Confronting Beauty, Pornography, and the Future of Feminism*. Berkeley: University of California Press.

Chapkis, Wendy. 1997. *Live Sex Acts: Women Performing Erotic Labor*. New York: Routledge.

Chaudhry, Neena, and Jasmine Tucker. 2017. "Let Her Learn: Stopping School Push-out." National Women's Law Center. Washington, DC.

Clinton, Hillary Rodham. 2017. *What Happened*. New York: Simon & Schuster.

Cohen, Claire. July 14, 2017. "Donald Trump Sexism Tracker: Every Offensive Comment in One Place." *Telegraph*. www.telegraph.co.uk.

Collins, Patricia Hill. 2000. *Black Feminist Thought: Knowledge, Consciousness, and the Politics of Empowerment*, 2nd ed. New York: Routledge.

———. 2004. *Black Sexual Politics: African Americans, Gender, and the New Racism*. New York: Routledge.

Connell, Raewyn. 1995. *Masculinities*. Berkeley: University of California Press.

Connell, Robert W., and James W. Messerschmidt. 2005. "Hegemonic Masculinity: Rethinking the Concept." *Gender & Society* 19(6): 829–859.

Conti, Allie. September 14, 2016. "How Many Racists Are There in America?" *Vice*. www.vice.com.

Currier, Danielle M. 2013. "Strategic Ambiguity: Protecting Emphasized Femininity and Hegemonic Masculinity in the Hookup Culture." *Gender & Society* 27(5): 704–727.

Daniels, Elizabeth A. 2016. "Sexiness on Social Media: The Social Costs of Using a Sexy Profile Photo." *Sexualization, Media, & Society* 2(4): 1–10.

Daniels, Jessie. 2018. "The Algorithmic Rise of the 'Alt-Right.'" *Contexts* 17(1): 60–65.

Davis, Angela Y. 1981. "Rape, Racism and the Myth of the Black Rapist." *Black Scholar* 12(6): 39–45.

Dean, James Joseph. 2014. *Straights: Heterosexuality in Post-closeted Culture*. New York: NYU Press.

De Beauvoir, Simone. 1952. *The Second Sex*. New York: Random House.

DeKeseredy, Walter S., and Martin D. Schwartz. 2016. "Thinking Sociologically about Image-Based Sexual Abuse: The Contribution of Male Peer Support Theory." *Sexualization, Media, & Society* 2(4). DOI: 2374623816684692.

Deuze, Mark. 2011. "Media Life." *Media, Culture & Society* 33(1): 137–148.

Dickson, E. J. September 22, 2017. "When Men Workshop Their Dick Pics." *The Cut*. www.thecut.com.

Diefendorf, Sarah. 2015. "After the Wedding Night: Sexual Abstinence and Masculinities over the Life Course." *Gender & Society* 29(5): 647–669.

Dines, Gail. 2006. "The White Man's Burden: Gonzo Pornography and the Construction of Black Masculinity." *Yale Journal of Law & Feminism* 18(1): 283–297.

———. 2010. *Pornland: How Porn Has Hijacked Our Sexuality*. Boston: Beacon Press.

Doane, Ashley W., and Eduardo Bonilla-Silva, eds. 2003. *White Out: The Continuing Significance of Race*. New York: Routledge.

Donoghue, Ngaire, Tim Kurtz, and Kally Whitehead. 2011. "Spinning the Pole: A Discursive Analysis of the Websites of Recreational Pole Dancing Studios." *Feminism & Psychology* 21(4): 443–457.

Douglas, Susan J. 2010. *Enlightened Sexism: The Seductive Message That Feminism's Work Is Done*. New York: Times Books.

Du Bois, W. E. B. 1903. *The Souls of Black Folk*. Chicago: A. C. McClurg & Co.

Duggan, Lisa, and Nan D. Hunter. 2006. *Sex Wars: Sexual Dissent and Political Culture*. New York: Routledge.

Dworkin, Andrea. 1974. *Woman Hating*. Boston: E. P. Dutton.

Egan, R. Danielle. 2013. *Becoming Sexual: A Critical Appraisal of the Sexualization of Girls*. Cambridge, UK: Polity Press.

Ehrenreich, John. May 7, 2018. "White Evangelicals' Continued Support of Trump Feels Surprising. It Shouldn't." *Slate*. http://slate.com.

Eligon, John. November 13, 2018. "Hate Crimes Increase for the Third Consecutive Year, F.B.I. Reports." *New York Times*. www.nytimes.com.

Eltahawy, Mona. 2015. *Headscarves and Hymens: Why the Middle East Needs a Sexual Revolution*. New York: Farrar, Straus & Giroux.

Engeln, Renee. 2017. *Beauty Sick: How the Cultural Obsession with Appearance Hurts Girls and Women*. New York: HarperCollins.

England, Paula, Emily Fitzgibbons Shafer, and Alison C. K. Fogarty. 2007. "Hooking Up and Forming Romantic Relationships on Today's College Campuses." In *The Gendered Society Reader*, 5th ed., edited by Michael Kimmel and Amy Aronson. New York: Oxford University Press, pp. 559–572.

Englander, Elisabeth K. 2015. "Coerced Sexting and Revenge Porn among Teens." *Bullying, Teen Aggression & Social Media* 1(2): 19–21.

Enloe, Cynthia. 2017. *The Big Push: Exposing and Challenging the Persistence of Patriarchy*. Oakland: University of California Press.

Erigha, Maryann. 2019. *The Hollywood Jim Crow: The Racial Politics of the Movie Industry*. New York: NYU Press.

Evans, Adrienne, Sarah Riley, and Avi Shanker. 2010. "Technologies of Sexiness: Theorizing Women's Engagement in the Sexualization of Culture." *Feminism & Psychology* 20(1): 114–131.

Fahrenthold, David A. October 8, 2016. "Trump Recorded Having Extremely Lewd Conversation about Women in 2005." *Washington Post*. www.washingtonpost.com.

Fahs, Breanne. 2014. "'Freedom to' and 'Freedom from': A New Vision for Sex-Positive Politics." *Sexualities* 17(3): 267–290.

Fea, John. 2018. *Believe Me: The Evangelical Road to Donald Trump*. Grand Rapids, MI: Eerdmans.

Ferber, Abby L. 2007. "Whiteness Studies and the Erasure of Gender." *Sociology Compass* 1(1): 265–282.

Fields, R. Douglas. January 26, 2016. "The Explosive Mix of Sex and Violence." *Psychology Today*. www.psychologytoday.com.

Fisher, Randy, Donna Derison, Chester F. Polley III, Jennifer Cadman, and Dana Johnston. 1994. "Religiousness, Religious Orientation, and Attitudes towards Gays and Lesbians." *Journal of Applied Social Psychology* 24(7): 614–630.

FitzGerald, Frances. 2017. *The Evangelicals: The Struggle to Shape America*. New York: Simon & Schuster.

Flynn, Gillian. 2014. *Gone Girl*. New York: Broadway Books.

Ford, Tanisha C. February 24, 2019. "What the 'Hollywood Jim Crow' Looks Like Today." *Atlantic*.

Fredrickson, Barbara L., and Tomi-Ann Roberts. 1997. "Objectification Theory: Toward Understanding Women's Lived Experiences and Mental Health Risks." *Psychology of Women Quarterly* 21(2): 173–206.

Freire, Paulo. 2018. *Pedagogy of the Oppressed*. New York: Bloomsbury Publishing.

Freitas. Donna. 2013. *The End of Sex: How Hookup Culture Is Leaving a Generation Unhappy, Sexually Unfulfilled, and Confused about Intimacy*. New York: Basic Books.

———. 2017. *The Happiness Effect: How Social Media Is Driving a Generation to Appear Perfect at Any Cost*. New York: Oxford University Press.

Freund, Kurt, and Ray Blanchard. 1986. "The Concept of Courtship Disorder." *Journal of Sex & Marital Therapy* 12(2): 79–92.

Fricker, Miranda. 2007. *Epistemic Injustice: Power and the Ethics of Knowing*. New York: Oxford University Press.

Friedman, Jaclyn. 2017. *Unscrewed: Women, Sex, Power, and How to Stop Letting the System Screw Us All*. New York: Seal Press.

Friedman, Thomas L. 2016. *Thank You for Being Late: An Optimist's Guide to Thriving in the Age of Accelerations*. London: Picador.

Fuller, Matt. May 20, 2016. "Donald Trump's Appearances on Howard Stern Tell You Everything You Need to Know about His Views on Women." *HuffPost*. www.huff post.com.

Galliano, Grace, Linda M. Noble, Linda A. Travis, and Carol Puechl. 1993. "Victim Reactions during Rape/Sexual Assault: A Preliminary Study of the Immobility Response and Its Correlates." *Journal of Interpersonal Violence* 8(1): 109–114.

Gerbner, George. 1967. "Mass Media and Human Communication Theory." In *Human Communication Theory: Original Essays*, edited by Frank E. X. Dance. New York: Holt, Rinehart & Winston, pp. 40–57.

Gill, Rosalind. 2007. "Postfeminist Media Culture: Elements of a Sensibility." *European Journal of Cultural Studies* 10(2): 147–166.

———. 2008. "Empowerment/Sexism: Figuring Female Sexual Agency in Contemporary Advertising." *Feminism & Psychology* 18(1): 35–60.

———. 2012. "Media Empowerment and the 'Sexualization of Culture' Debates." *Sex Roles* 66: 736–745.

Glick, Peter, and Susan T. Fiske. 1996. "The Ambivalent Sexism Inventory: Differentiating Hostile and Benevolent Sexism." *Journal of Personality and Social Psychology* 70(3): 491–512.

Goffman, Erving. 1959. *The Presentation of Self in Everyday Life*. New York: Anchor Books.

———. 1979. *Gender Advertisements*. New York: Macmillan International Higher Education.

Goled, Shraddha. February 22, 2019. "'Show Me Your Strength by Lifting Somebody Up': Obama Busts Myths around Masculinity." *Logical Indian*.

Gose, Leah, and Theda Skocpol. 2018. "Resist, Persist, and Transform: The Emergence and Impact of Grassroots Resistance Groups in the Early Trump Presidency." Paper presented at the American Sociological Association Annual Meeting, Philadelphia.

Gunning, Sandra. 1996. *Race, Rape, and Lynching: The Red Record of American Literature, 1890–1912*. New York: Oxford University Press.

Hall, Stuart. 2000. "Racist Ideologies and the Media." In *Media Studies: A Reader*, 2nd ed., edited by Paul Marris and Sue Thornham. New York: NYU Press, pp. 271–82.

Hamilton, Laura. 2007. "Trading on Heterosexuality: College Women's Gender Strategies and Homophobia." *Gender & Society* 21(2): 145–172.

Harding, Luke. 2017. *Collusion: Secret Meetings, Dirty Money, and How Russia Helped Donald Trump Win*. New York: Vintage Books.

Hayes, Rebecca M., and Molly Dragiewicz. 2018. "Unsolicited Dick Pics: Erotica, Exhibitionism or Entitlement?" *Women's Studies International Forum* 71: 114–120.

Henley, Nancy, and Fred Pincus. 1978. "Interrelationship of Sexist, Racist, and Antihomosexual Attitudes." *Psychological Reports* 42: 83–90.

Herbenick, Debby, Jessamyn Bowling, Tsung-Chieh Jane Fu, Brian Dodge, Lucia Guerra-Reyes, and Stephanie Sanders. 2017. "Sexual Diversity in the United States: Results from a Nationally Representative Probability Sample of Adult Women and Men." *PloS one* 12(7): e0181198.

Herek, Gregory. 1987. "Religious Orientation and Prejudice: A Comparison of Racial and Sexual Attitudes." *Personality and Social Psychology Bulletin* 13(1): 34–44.

Herzog, Dagmar. 2008. *Sex in Crisis: The New Sexual Revolution and the Future of American Politics*. New York: Perseus Books.

Hlavka, Heather R. 2014. "Normalizing Sexual Violence: Young Women Account for Harassment and Abuse." *Gender & Society* 28(3): 337–358.

Hochschild, Arlie Russell. 2018. *Strangers in Their Own Land: Anger and Mourning on the American Right*. New York: New Press.

Hochschild, Arlie Russell, and Anne Machung. 2012. *The Second Shift: Working Families and the Revolution at Home*. New York: Penguin Books.

Hodes, Martha. 2014. *White Women, Black Men*. New Haven, CT: Yale University Press.

Holland, Samantha, and Feona Attwood. 2009. "Keeping Fit in Six Inch Heels: The Mainstreaming of Pole Dancing." In *Mainstreaming Sex: The Sexualization of Western Culture*, edited by Feona Attwood. London and New York: I.B. Tauris & Co., pp. 165–181.

hooks, bell. 1989. *Talking Back: Thinking Feminist, Thinking Black*. Boston: South End Press.

———. February 1994. "Sexism and Misogyny: Who Takes the Rap?" *Z Magazine*.

Horowitz, Juliana Menasce, Anna Brown, and Kiana Cox. April 9, 2019. "Race in America 2019." Pew Research Center. Washington, DC.

Hunter, Margaret, and Kathleen Soto. 2009. "Women of Color in Hip Hop: The Pornographic Gaze." *Race, Gender & Class* 16(1): 170–191.

Hurt, Byron, dir. 2006. *Hip Hop: Beyond Beats & Rhymes*. Media Education Foundation.

Hurtado, Aida. 1989. "Relating to Privilege: Seduction and Rejection in the Subordination of White Women and Women of Color." *Signs: Journal of Women in Culture and Society* 14(4): 833–855.

Ingraham, Chrys, and Casey Saunders. 2016. "Heterosexual Imaginary." In *The Wiley Blackwell Encyclopedia of Gender and Sexuality Studies*, edited by Nancy A. Naples, J. Michael Ryan, renée c. hoogland, Maithree Wickramasing, and Wai Ching Angela Wong. Wiley-Blackwell. DOI: 10.1002/9781118663219.

Jamieson, Kathleen Hall. 2018. *Cyberwar: How Russian Hackers and Trolls Helped Elect a President—What We Don't, Can't, and Do Know*. New York: Oxford University Press.

Jane, Emma A. 2015. "Flaming? What Flaming? The Pitfalls and Potentials of Researching Online Hostility." *Ethics and Information Technology* 17(1): 65–87.

Jensen, Robert. 2007. *Getting Off: Pornography and the End of Masculinity*. Boston: South End Press.

Jhally, Sut, dir. 2008. *Dreamworlds 3: Desire, Sex & Power in Music Videos*. Media Education Foundation.

———. 2009. *The Codes of Gender: Identity & Performance in Popular Culture*. Media Education Foundation.

———. 2010. *Killing Us Softly 4*. Media Education Foundation.

Johnson, Allan. 2006. *Privilege, Power and Difference*. New York: McGraw Hill.

Jones, Angela. April 13, 2020. "Rule 34 in Action: Coronavirus Porn, Satire, and Survival." *Medium*. https://medium.com.

Kamenetz, Anya. October 19, 2017. "Young Children Are Spending Much More Time in front of Small Screens." *NPR*. www.npr.org.

Kandiyoti, Deniz. 1988. "Bargaining with Patriarchy." *Gender & Society* 2(3): 274–290.

Katz, Jackson. 2016. *Man Enough?: Donald Trump, Hillary Clinton, and the Politics of Presidential Masculinity*. Northampton, MA: Interlink Books.

Keith, Thomas, dir. 2008. *Generation M: Misogyny in Media & Culture.* Media Education Foundation.

Kilday, Gregg. January 3, 2019. "Study: Women Film Directors Saw Their Numbers Shrink in 2018." *Hollywood Reporter.* www.hollywoodreporter.com.

Kimmel, Michael. 2017. *Angry White Men: American Masculinity at the End of an Era.* New York: Nation Books.

King, A. L. S., A. M. Valença, A. C. O. Silva, T. Baczynski, M. R. Carvalho, and A. E. Nardi. 2013. "Nomophobia: Dependency on Virtual Environments or Social Phobia?" *Computers in Human Behavior* 29(1): 140–144.

Kirkpatrick, Lee. 1993. "Fundamentalism, Christian Orthodoxy, and Intrinsic Religious Orientation as Predictors of Discriminatory Attitudes." *Journal for the Scientific Study of Religion* 32(3): 256–268.

Klaassen, Abbey. June 22, 2010. "Diesel Wins Outdoor Grand Prix for 'Be Stupid.'" *Ad Age.* http://adage.com.

Kohut, Taylor, William A. Fisher, and Lorne Campbell. 2017. "Perceived Effects of Pornography on the Couple Relationship: Initial Findings of Open-Ended, Participant-Informed, 'Bottom-Up' Research." *Archives of Sexual Behavior* 46(2): 585–602.

Kohn, Isabelle. October 30, 2018. "Guys Explain Why They Send Dick Pics and Girls Tell Us What They Think of Them." *Rooster.* http://therooster.com.

Kreager, Derek A., and Jeremy Staff. 2009. "The Sexual Double Standard and Adolescent Peer Acceptance." *Social Psychology Quarterly* 72(2): 143–164.

Kuruvilla, Carol. April 4, 2018. "Researchers Discover Common Threads among Christians Who Voted for Trump." *HuffPost.* www.huffpost.com.

Landsbaum, Claire. December 8, 2016. "Donald Trump's Pick for Labor Secretary Defended His Company's Sexist Ads." *The Cut.* www.thecut.com.

Laythe, Brian, Deborah Finkel, and Lee A. Kirkpatrick. 2001. "Predicting Prejudice from Religious Fundamentalism and Right-Wing Authoritarianism: A Multiple-Regression Approach." *Journal for the Scientific Study of Religion* 40(1): 1–10.

Lazarus, Margaret, dir. 2000. *Beyond Killing Us Softly.* Cambridge Documentary Films.

Lebowitz, Shana. September 10, 2016. "The Vast Majority of Tinder Users Aren't Using the App the Way You Might Expect." *Business Insider.* htttp://finance.yahoo.com.

Lee, Peter. March 25, 2016. "Learning from Tay's Introduction." *Official Microsoft Blog.* http://blogs.microsoft.com.

Lerner, Gerda. 1986. *The Creation of Patriarchy.* New York: Oxford University Press.

Levey, Tania G. 2018. *Sexual Harassment Online: Shaming and Silencing Women in the Digital Age.* Boulder, CO: Lynne Rienner Publishers.

Levy, Ariel. 2005. *Female Chauvinist Pigs: Women and the Rise of Raunch Culture.* New York: Free Press.

Lewis, Philip. August 28, 2018. "Vermont's Only Black Woman Lawmaker Pulls Out of Race in Wake of Online Threats." *HuffPost.* www.huffpost.com.

Ley, David, Nicole Prause, and Peter Finn. 2014. "The Emperor Has No Clothes: A Review of the 'Pornography Addiction' Model." *Current Sexual Health Reports* 6(2): 94–105.

Lovejoy, Meg. 2012. "Is Hooking Up Empowering for College Women? A Feminist Gramscian Perspective." PhD dissertation, Brandeis University.

Lukianoff, Greg, and Jonathan Haidt. 2018. *The Coddling of the American Mind: How Good Intentions and Bad Ideas Are Setting Up a Generation for Failure*. New York: Penguin Books.

Lumsden, Karen, and Heather M. Morgan. 2012. "'Fraping,' 'Sexting,' 'Trolling,' and 'Rinsing': Social Networking, Feminist Thought and the Construction of Young Women as Victims or Villains." https://dspace.lboro.ac.uk/2134/15756.

Lyubomirsky, Sonja. 2013. *The Myths of Happiness: What Should Make You Happy, but Doesn't, What Shouldn't Make You Happy, but Does*. New York: Penguin Books.

Madigan, Sheri, Anh Ly, Christina L. Rash, Joris Van Ouytsel, and Jeff R. Temple. 2018. "Prevalence of Multiple Forms of Sexting Behavior among Youth: A Systematic Review and Meta-Analysis." *JAMA Pediatrics* 172(4): 327–335.

Mandau, Morten Birk Hansen. 2019. "'Directly in Your Face': A Qualitative Study on the Sending and Receiving of Unsolicited 'Dick Pics' among Young Adults." *Sexuality & Culture* 24: 72–93.

Manne, Kate. 2017. *Down Girl: The Logic of Misogyny*. New York: Oxford University Press.

Manza, Jeff, and Ned Crowley. 2018. "Ethnonationalism and the Rise of Donald Trump." *Contexts* 17(1): 28–33.

Marwick, Alice E., and danah boyd. 2011. "I Tweet Honestly, I Tweet Passionately: Twitter Users, Context Collapse, and the Imagined Audience." *New Media & Society* 13(1): 114–133.

May, Gareth. February 25, 2015. "Why Is Incest Porn So Popular?" *Vice*. www.vice.com.

McCullough, Brian. January 4, 2015. "Chapter 6—A History of Internet Porn." *Internet History Podcast*, www.internethistorypodcast.com.

McIntosh, Peggy. 2007. "White Privilege and Male Privilege." In *Women's Voices, Feminist Visions: Classic and Contemporary Readings*, edited by Susan M. Shaw and Janet Lee. New York: McGraw Hill, pp. 91–98.

McLaurin, Melton Alonza. 1991. *Celia: A Slave*. Athens: University of Georgia Press.

McNair, Brian. 2002. *Striptease Culture: Sex, Media and the Democratization of Desire*. New York: Routledge.

———. 2009. "From Porn Chic to Porn Fear: The Return of the Repressed." In *Mainstreaming Sex: The Sexualization of Western Culture*, edited by Feona Attwood. London and New York: I.B. Tauris & Co., pp. 55–73.

McRobbie, Angela. 2008. *The Aftermath of Feminism: Gender, Culture and Social Change*. Los Angeles and London: Sage.

Meyer, David. March 30, 2016. "Microsoft's Tay 'AI' Bot Returns, Disastrously." *Fortune*. http://fortune.com.

Mindock, Clark. May 23, 2018. "Startling Increase in Physical and Sexual Abuse of Child Immigrants by US Border Patrol, New Report Alleges." *Independent*. www .independent.co.uk.

Modi, Radha. 2018. "Communities on Fire: Confronting Hate Violence and Xenophobic Political Rhetoric." SAALT (South Asian Americans Leading Together). Takoma Park, MD.

Möller, Anna, Hans Peter Söndergaard, and Lotti Helström. 2017. "Tonic Immobility during Sexual Assault—a Common Reaction Predicting Post-Traumatic Stress Disorder and Severe Depression." *Acta Obstetricia et Gynecologica Scandinavica* 96(8): 932–938.

Moraga, Cherríe, and Gloria Anzaldúa, eds. 2015. *This Bridge Called My Back: Writings by Radical Women of Color*. Albany: SUNY Press.

Morgan, Robin. 1970. *Sisterhood Is Powerful: An Anthology of Writings from the Women's Liberation Movement*. New York: Vintage Books.

Mulvey, Laura. 1975. "Visual Pleasure and Narrative Cinema." *Screen* 16: 6–18.

Myers, Jessica. November 30, 2017. "Finstas Are the New Rinstas: An Increasing Number of Instagram Users Are Making Second Accounts." *State Press*. www.statepress .com.

Nestle, Joan, ed. 1992. *The Persistent Desire: A Butch Femme Reader*. Boston: Alyson Publications.

Newsom, Jennifer Siebel, dir. 2011. *Miss Representation*. Girls' Club Entertainment.

Noble, Safiya Umoja. 2018. *Algorithms of Oppression: How Search Engines Reinforce Racism*. New York: NYU Press.

North, Anna. December 5, 2018. "Report: How Les Moonves Avoided Consequences for Sexual Misconduct Allegations for So Long." *Vox*. www.vox.com.

Olmstead, Spencer B., Sesen Negash, Kay Pasley, and Frank D. Fincham. 2013. "Emerging Adults' Expectations for Pornography Use in the Context of Future Committed Romantic Relationships: A Qualitative Study." *Archives of Sexual Behavior* 42(4): 625–635.

O'Neill, Sean P. 2015. "Sapir–Whorf Hypothesis." In *The International Encyclopedia of Language and Social Interaction*, edited by Karen Tracy, Cornelia Ilie, and Todd Sandel. Wiley-Blackwell/ICA. DOI: 10.1002/9781118611463.

Oppliger, Patrice A. 2008. *Girls Gone Skank: The Sexualization of Girls in American Culture*. Jefferson, NC, and London: McFarland.

O'Reilly, Michelle, Nisha Dogra, Natasha Whiteman, Jason Hughes, Seyda Eruyar, and Paul Reilly. 2018. "Is Social Media Bad for Mental Health and Wellbeing? Exploring the Perspectives of Adolescents." *Clinical Child Psychology and Psychiatry* 23(4): 601–613.

Orenstein, Peggy. 2016. *Girls & Sex: Navigating the Complicated New Landscape*. New York: HarperCollins.

Paasonen, Susanna. 2011. "Online Pornography: Ubiquitous and Effaced." In *The Handbook of Internet Studies*, edited by Mia Consalvo and Charles Ess. Wiley-Blackwell. DOI: 10.1002/9781444314861.

Palmer, Maureen, dir. 2012. *Sext Up Kids*. Media Education Foundation.

Park, Brian Y., Gary Wilson, Jonathan Berger, Matthew Christman, Bryn Reina, Frank Bishop, Warren P. Klam, and Andrew P. Doan. 2016. "Is Internet Pornography Causing Sexual Dysfunctions? A Review with Clinical Reports." *Behavioral Sciences* 6(3): 17.

Paul, Pamela. 2005. *Pornified: How Pornography Is Damaging Our Lives, Our Relationships, and Our Families*. New York: Henry Holt.

Parlapiano, Alicia, and Jasmine C. Lee. February 16, 2018. "The Propaganda Tools Used by Russians to Influence the 2016 Election." *New York Times*. www.nytimes.com.

Perry, Richard Warren, and Lisa Erin Sanchez. 1998. "Transactions in the Flesh: Toward an Ethnography of Embodied Sexual Reason." *Studies in Law, Politics, and Society* 18: 29–76.

Pharr, Suzanne. 1996. *In the Time of the Right: Reflections on Liberation*. Berkeley, CA: Chardon Press.

Phillips, Lynn. 2000. *Flirting with Danger: Young Women's Reflections on Sexuality and Domination*. New York: NYU Press.

Phillips, Whitney. 2015. *This Is Why We Can't Have Nice Things: Mapping the Relationship between Online Trolling and Mainstream Culture*. Cambridge, MA: MIT Press.

Picker, Miguel, and Chyng Sun, dirs. 2012. *Latinos beyond Reel*. Media Education Foundation.

Pinker, Steven. 2011. *The Better Angels of Our Nature: Why Violence Has Declined*. New York: Penguin Books.

Poland, Bailey. 2016. *Haters: Harassment, Abuse, and Violence Online*. Lincoln: University of Nebraska Press.

Pollet, Alison, and Page Hurwitz. December 24, 2003. "Strip till You Drop." *Nation*. www.thenation.com.

Pollitt, Katha. March 22, 2018. "Why Evangelicals—Still!—Support Trump." *Nation*. www.thenation.com.

Potter, W. James. 2004. "Argument for the Need for a Cognitive Theory of Media Literacy." *American Behavioral Scientist* 48(2): 266–272.

———. 2014. "A Critical Analysis of Cultivation Theory." *Journal of Communication* 64(6): 1015–1036.

Primack, Brian A., Ariel Shensa, César G. Escobar-Viera, Erica L. Barrett, Jaime E. Sidani, Jason B. Colditz, and A. Everette James. 2017. "Use of Multiple Social Media Platforms and Symptoms of Depression and Anxiety: A Nationally Representative Study among US Young Adults." *Computers in Human Behavior* 69: 1–9.

Queen, Carol, and Lynn Comella. 2008. "The Necessary Revolution: Sex-Positive Feminism in the Post-Barnard Era." *Communication Review* 11(3): 274–291.

Relman, Eliza. June 21, 2019. "The 24 Women Who Have Accused Trump of Sexual Misconduct." *Business Insider*. www.businessinsider.com.

Resnikoff, Paul. January 20, 2014. "The Music Industry: It's Still a White Boys' Club." *Digital Music News*. www.digitalmusicnews.com.

Ringrose, Jessica, Laura Harvey, Rosalind Gill, and Sonia Livingstone. 2013. "Teen Girls, Sexual Double Standards and 'Sexting': Gendered Value in Digital Image Exchange." *Feminist Theory* 14(3): 305–323.

Romero, Mary. 2018. "Trump's Immigration Attacks, in Brief." *Contexts* 17(1): 34–41.

Ronen, Shelly. 2010. "Grinding on the Dance Floor: Gendered Scripts and Sexualized Dancing at College Parties." *Gender & Society* 24(3): 355–377.

Rothman, Emily F., Courtney Kaczmarsky, Nina Burke, Emily Jansen, and Allyson Baughman. 2015. "'Without Porn . . . I Wouldn't Know Half the Things I Know Now': A Qualitative Study of Pornography Use among a Sample of Urban, Low-Income, Black and Hispanic Youth." *Journal of Sex Research* 52(7): 736–746.

Rushkoff, Douglas. 2013. *Present Shock: When Everything Happens Now*. New York: Penguin Books.

Sabina, Chiara, Janis Wolak, and David Finkelhor. 2008. "The Nature and Dynamics of Internet Pornography Exposure for Youth." *CyberPsychology & Behavior* 11(6): 691–693.

Sales, Nancy Jo. 2016. *American Girls: Social Media and the Secret Lives of Teenagers*. New York: Alfred A. Knopf.

Salim, Saima. January 4, 2019. "How Much Time Do You Spend on Social Media? Research Says 142 Minutes a Day." *Digital Information World*. www.digitalinformationworld.com.

Salter, Michael. 2016. "Privates in the Online Public: Sex(ting) and Reputation on Social Media." *New Media & Society* 18(11): 2723–2739.

Sanson, Mevagh, Deryn Strange, and Maryanne Garry. 2019. "Trigger Warnings Are Trivially Helpful at Reducing Negative Affect, Intrusive Thoughts, and Avoidance." *Clinical Psychological Science* 7(4): 778–793.

Santelli, John S., Leslie M. Kantor, Stephanie A. Grilo, Ilene S. Speizer, Laura D. Lindberg, Jennifer Heitel, and Amy T. Schalet. 2017. "Abstinence-Only-until-Marriage: An Updated Review of US Policies and Programs and Their Impact." *Journal of Adolescent Health* 61(3): 273–280.

Schippers, Mimi. 2007. "Recovering the Feminine Other: Masculinity, Femininity, and Gender Hegemony." *Theory and Society* 36: 85–102.

Segran, Elizabeth, and Kimberly Truong. April 18, 2016. "Real Dick-Pic Senders Explain Why They Do It." *Refinery29*. www.refinery29.com.

Sheets, Megan. May 24, 2019. "Harvard Student Magazine Is Slammed for 'Deeply Offensive' Image of Anne Frank's Face Super-imposed over Heidi Montag's Post-plastic Surgery Body in a Bikini." *DailyMail.com*. www.dailymail.co.uk.

Singer, Maya. February 8, 2017. "How Models Like Ashley Graham and Gigi Hadid Are Democratizing Fashion." *Vogue*. www.vogue.com.

Smith, Stacy L., Marc Choueiti, and Katherine Pieper. 2016. "Inclusion or Invisibility? Comprehensive Annenberg Report on Diversity in Entertainment." Institute for

Diversity and Empowerment at Annenberg (IDEA), USC Annenberg School of Communication and Journalism. Los Angeles.

Snow, Aurora. April 22, 2017. "'Fauxcest': The Disturbing Rise of Incest-Themed Porn." *Daily Beast.* www.thedailybeast.com.

Snyder, Timothy. 2018. *The Road to Unfreedom.* New York: Tim Duggan Books.

Solnit, Rebecca. November 4, 2018. "The American Civil War Didn't End. And Trump Is a Confederate President." *Guardian.* www.theguardian.com.

Starhawk. 1993. *The Fifth Sacred Thing.* New York: Bantam.

Stewart, Destin N., and Dawn M. Szymanski. 2012. "Young Adult Women's Reports of Their Male Romantic Partner's Pornography Use as a Correlate of Their Self-Esteem, Relationship Quality, and Sexual Satisfaction." *Sex Roles* 67(5–6): 257–271.

Suellentrop, Chris. October 25, 2014. "The Disheartening GamerGate Campaign." *New York Times.* www.nytimes.com.

Suler, John. 2004. "The Online Disinhibition Effect." *CyberPsychology & Behavior* 7(3): 321–326.

Sun, Chyng, Ana Bridges, Jennifer A. Johnson, and Matthew B. Ezzell. 2016. "Pornography and the Male Sexual Script: An Analysis of Consumption and Sexual Relations." *Archives of Sexual Behavior* 45(4): 983–994.

Sun, Chyng, and Miguel Picker, dirs. 2001. *Mickey Mouse Monopoly: Disney, Childhood & Corporate Power.* Media Education Foundation.

———. 2008. *The Price of Pleasure: Pornography, Sexuality & Relationships.* Media Education Foundation.

Tanenbaum, Leora. 2015. *I Am Not a Slut: Slut-Shaming in the Age of the Internet.* New York: Harper.

Tolman, Deborah L. 2002. *Dilemmas of Desire: Teenage Girls Talk about Sexuality.* Cambridge, MA, and London: Harvard University Press.

Tromholt, Morten. 2016. "The Facebook Experiment: Quitting Facebook Leads to Higher Levels of Well-Being." *Cyberpsychology, Behavior, and Social Networking* 19(11): 661–666.

Turel, Ofir, Daniel Cavagnaro, and Dar Meshi. 2018. "Short Abstinence from Online Social Networking Sites Reduces Perceived Stress, Especially in Excessive Users." *Psychiatry Research* 270: 947–953.

Turkle, Sherry. 2015. *Reclaiming Conversation: The Power of Talk in a Digital Age.* New York: Penguin Books.

Twenge, Jean M., Ryne A. Sherman, and Brooke E. Wells. 2017. "Sexual Inactivity during Young Adulthood Is More Common among US Millennials and iGen: Age, Period, and Cohort Effects on Having No Sexual Partners after Age 18." *Archives of Sexual Behavior* 46(2): 433–440.

Valdes, Francisco. 1996. "Unpacking Hetero-Patriarchy: Tracing the Conflation of Sex, Gender & Sexual Orientation to Its Origins." *Yale Journal of Law & the Humanities* 8(1): 161–211.

Vance, Carol S., ed. 1984. *Pleasure and Danger: Exploring Female Sexuality*. Boston: Routledge & Kegan Paul.

Veiga Mateos, Jaime, and Joshua Saxon. February 20, 2017. "Why Your Customers' Attention Is the Scarcest Resource in 2017." *Research World*. www.research world.com.

Vogel, Erin A., Jason P. Rose, Lindsay R. Roberts, and Katheryn Eckles. 2014. "Social Comparison, Social Media, and Self-Esteem." *Psychology of Popular Media Culture* 3(4): 206–222.

Wade, Lisa. 2017. *American Hookup: The New Culture of Sex on Campus*. New York: W. W. Norton & Co.

Ward, Jane. 2015. *Not Gay: Sex between Straight White Men*. New York: NYU Press.

———. 2020. *The Tragedy of Heterosexuality*. New York: NYU Press.

Walter, Natasha. 2015. *Living Dolls: The Return of Sexism*. London: Virago Press.

Wesley, Jennifer. 2012. *Being Female: The Continuum of Sexualization*. Boulder, CO: Lynne Rienner Publishers.

West, Lindy. February 2, 2015. "What Happened When I Confronted My Cruellest Troll." *Guardian*. www.theguardian.com.

Whitehead, Andrew L., Samuel L. Perry, and Joseph O. Baker. 2018. "Make America Christian Again: Christian Nationalism and Voting for Donald Trump in the 2016 Presidential Election." *Sociology of Religion* 79(2): 147–171.

Whitley, Bernard. 1999. "Right-Wing Authoritarianism, Social Dominance Orientation, and Prejudice." *Journal of Personality and Social Psychology* 77(1): 126–134.

Whitley, Bernard, and Stefania Egisdottir. 2000. "The Gender Belief System, Authoritarianism, Social Dominance Orientation, and Heterosexuals' Attitudes toward Lesbians and Gay Men." *Sex Roles* 42(11/12): 947–967.

Whitley, Bernard, and Sarah E. Lee. 2000. "The Relationship of Authoritarianism and Related Constructs to Attitudes toward Homosexuality." *Journal of Applied Social Psychology* 30(1): 144–170.

Wilson, Gary. May 16, 2012. "The Great Porn Experiment: Gary Wilson at TEDxGlasgow." www.youtube.com/watch?v=wSF82AwSDiU.

Wilson-Hartgrove, Jonathan. February 16, 2018. "Why Evangelicals Support President Trump, Despite His Immorality." *Time*. http://time.com.

Withnall, Adam. October 10, 2016. "Donald Trump's Unsettling Record of Comments about His Daughter Ivanka." *Independent*. www.independent.co.uk.

Wolf, Naomi. 1991. *The Beauty Myth: How Images of Beauty Are Used against Women*. New York: Anchor.

Woods, Heather Cleland, and Holly Scott. 2016. "#Sleepyteens: Social Media Use in Adolescence Is Associated with Poor Sleep Quality, Anxiety, Depression and Low Self-Esteem." *Journal of Adolescence* 51: 41–49.

Worthen, Molly. May 2017. "A Match Made in Heaven: Why Conservative Evangelicals Have Lined Up behind Trump." *Atlantic*. www.theatlantic.com.

Yoon, Sunkyung, Mary Kleinman, Jessica Mertz, and Michael Brannick. 2019. "Is Social Network Site Usage Related to Depression? A Meta-analysis of Facebook-Depression Relations." *Journal of Affective Disorders* 248: 65–72.

Zickl, Danielle. August 14, 2017. "AirDropping Dick Pics Is Now a Thing, and People Are Horrified." *Men's Health*. www.menshealth.com.

INDEX

Page numbers in *italics* refer to figures.

abstinence-only sexual education, 24, 163, 188n7

Abu Ghraib, 169

Access Hollywood (television show), 141

action films, 33

actors of color, 35

addiction, 182n29

African Americans, 22

aggrieved entitlement, 9, 118

Aladdin (1992), *42*

Amazon, 128

American Apparel, *46*

American Horror Story (television show), 4

American Pie (film series), 38

"Anaconda" (Minaj), *45*

anal sex, 63, 66, 181n19

Anderson, Pamela, 5, *43*

andro-privilege, 179n28

androsexism, 49, 50, 53, 97, 104

anonymity, 108

antebellum South, 22

anti-immigrant rhetoric, 185n12

anti-pornography activists, 17

anti-pornography books, 162

anxiety, 92

AVN Adult Entertainment Expo, 62

Azar, 184n1

Babes for Trump, 133, *134*, 136

Baby Boomers, 79; dick pics and, 114

Bad Reality, 147–48

Bailey, Moya, 36

Barber, Kristen, 180n32

Barb Wire (1996), *43*

"basket of deplorables" speech (Clinton), 144

beauty culture, 94

beauty obsessions, 91

benevolent sexism, 145

benign disinhibition, 184n2

Berger, John, 178n2

BetweenTheSheets.com, 139

Bible Belt, 163

bigotry, 143, 144

Bilzerian, Dan, *47*

birth control, 10, 116, 163

black men, depictions of, 37

Bloodworth-Thomason, Linda, 178n7

Blue Mountain State (television show), 31, *32*, 33

"Blurred Lines" (Thicke), *45*

bodily autonomy, 151, 172

body image issues, 92; creation of, 23; social media and, 95, 122

body shaming, 104–5, 106

Bordo, Susan, 188n47

breakups, 88

broadcast television, 75

bro-culture, 24

bro-privilege, 48–50, 52, 53, 179n28, 180n41

Brown, Helen Gurley, 25

Brzezinski, Mika, 131

bukkake, 64, 65, 181n22

ABOUT THE AUTHOR

Bernadette Barton is Professor of Sociology and Director of Gender Studies at Morehead State University in Morehead, Kentucky. Her books include *Stripped: More Stories from Exotic Dancers* and *Pray the Gay Away: The Extraordinary Lives of Bible Belt Gays.*